DOCTORS . . .

It must be wonderful to be one. What other job lets you ask a girl to take off her clothes—and send the bill to her husband?

LARRY WILDE'S THE OFFICIAL DOCTORS JOKE BOOK

Hundreds of jokes that will have you in stitches . . . about doctors, quacks, shrinks, surgeons, dentists, nurses, interns . . . and patients, too.

THE OFFICIAL DOCTORS JOKEBOOK

Larry Wilde

Illustrations by Ron Wing

BANTAM BOOKS
TORONTO · NEW YORK · LONDON

THE OFFICIAL DOCTORS JOKE BOOK
A Bantam Book/July 1981

ISBN 0-553-14751-X

Published simultaneously in the United States and Canada

Bantam Books are published by Bantam Books, Inc. Its trademark, consisting
of the words "Bantam Books" and the portrayal of a bantam, is Registered
in U.S. Patent and Trademark Office and in other countries. Marca Registrada.
Bantam Books, Inc., 666 Fifth Avenue, New York, New York 10103.

PRINTED IN THE UNITED STATES OF AMERICA

0 9 8 7 6 5 4 3 2 1

The Lord and the Doctor we alike adore
But on the brink of danger, not before.
When the danger has passed, both are alike
  requited—
The Lord is forgotten, the Doctor slighted.

DEDICATED TO:

*Harold Bieber, the Jersey City physician,
surgeon, sportsman, bon vivant,
and lover of mankind.*

CONTENTS

THE
OFFICIAL
DOCTORS
JOKEBOOK

Introduction

Sickness soaks the purse.
Better a lucky physician than a learned one.
The doctor is to be more feared than the disease.

So spoke the Romans over 2000 years ago, and there are many citizens today who would heartily agree. Poking fun at the medical profession is a time-honored practice. The following exchange plucked from the pages of history provides a typical account of medical persiflage:

Plutarch, the Greek biographer, was a well-known hypochondriac. One morning he shouted to a servant, "Get me an undertaker!"

"But, master," said the slave, "you mean a physician."

"No," replied Plutarch. "I am eliminating the middleman."

1

Why should these saviors of humanity suffer such biting satire? What makes them so especially vulnerable to poison tongues? Perhaps the answer lies in still another question:

What is the difference between an itch and an allergy?
About $25 a visit.

Napoleon was known to be fascinated by psychic phenomena. He put more trust in that form of healing than in any of his medical advisers. When pressed to explain his reasons, he said:

Medicine is a collection of uncertain prescriptions, the results of which, taken collectively, are more fatal than useful to mankind.

Since the Angel of Death hovers near all those who live, the fear of the doctor bringing him closer is ever present. What else to do but joke about it?

Nugent was being examined for some insurance by the company physician. The M.D. asked about his family history.
"Did your father die a natural death?" he inquired.
"Oh, no," answered Nugent. "He had a doctor!"

Of course, the surgeon must stand responsible for his work since he very often holds life in his hands. Should he fail in his performance, he has to face judgment by his fellowman. Sometimes humorously:

A country doctor stopped in at the small town general store. "Mornin', Doc," said the owner. "Where ya been?"

"Oh, I was up North for a week of hunting."

"Kill anything?"

"Not a darned thing," said the M.D.

"Gollee," said the storekeeper. "You could've done better'n that stayin' home and tendin' to your regular trade."

Becoming a doctor has long been looked up to as the height of social accomplishment. Medicine is considered the most prestigious of all professions, particularly so in Jewish cultures. Witness this tale:

Sister Margaret Alice, a Catholic nun, died and arrived at the Pearly Gates. "You've been a model of the church," said St. Peter. "Is there anything special we can offer you?"

"Yes," replied the nun. "I've always admired the Virgin Mary. Could I meet her?"

St. Peter led her to another cloud. There

sat a gray-haired lady in a rocking chair knitting. "Oh, Blessed Virgin, what a joy to meet you!" exclaimed the nun. "How does it feel to be the mother of God?"

And Mary replied, "Poisonally, I wanted he should become a doctor!"

Whether you are for or agin' the Hippocratic healers isn't really as important as being able to laugh about them. Even the medics prescribe a good guffaw to break daily tensions. The following pages contain a collection of the best gags and quips and stories associated with every facet of the medical world.

So get yourself comfortable. Forget the boss and the mortgage and the crab grass and try to relax. Maybe by chuckling over doctors you won't have to visit one. After all, laughter is still the best medicine.

LARRY WILDE
Los Angeles

Comic Comments

oking fun at pill pushers has always provoked loud guffaws for America's court jesters. Audiences seem to delight in hearing comedians make light of such a serious subject as medicine. Here are some oft quoted classic quips from the lips of the country's top comedy practitioners:

A rule of thumb in the matter of medical advice is to take everything any doctor says with a grain of aspirin.

—GOODMAN ACE

I realized after $25,000 worth of analysis that if I'd had that $25,000 in the first place, I wouldn't have needed the analysis.

—WOODY ALLEN

It must be wonderful to be a doctor. In what other job could you ask a girl to take her clothes off, look her over at your leisure—then send the bill to her husband?

—MARTY ALLEN

My doctor is terrific! Some doctors will treat you for a broken arm and you'll die of pneumonia. If my doctor treats you for a broken arm, you die of a broken arm.

—MOREY AMSTERDAM

I asked the nurse, "Does this doctor ever make house calls?"

She said, "Yeah, what time can you be at his house?"

I said to the doctor, "I have this ringing in my ears." He said, "Don't answer it."

—JOEY BISHOP

My doctor told me to stop smoking. Then he said, "And since you're quitting, I'll give you five dollars for your gold lighter."

—PAT COOPER

I once had an unusual doctor. He told me I had walking pneumonia, and he charged me by the mile.

—RODNEY DANGERFIELD

I go to a family physician. He treats mine and I support his.

—PHYLLIS DILLER

All my doctor does is make appointments for me to see another doctor. I'm not sure if he is really a physician or a booking agent.

My doctor specializes in acupuncture— that wonderful healing method developed by Don Rickles.

—BOB HOPE

The other day my doctor told me I had low blood pressure, but he promptly gave me something to raise it—his bill.

—ALAN KING

My doctor said I was sound as a dollar. That scared the hell out of me.

—RED SKELTON

My doctor is a wonderful man. He gave a guy six months to live. The fellow couldn't pay his bill, so he gave him another six months.

—HENNY YOUNGMAN

At the Mort Fleischmann Testimonial Dinner in Hollywood the following excerpt of dialogue was done by the author and Jose Jimenez (played by his creator, Bill Dana):

Wilde: What else have you done for a living?

Jose: I was a doctor . . . a geneologist.

Wilde: You don't mean geneologist . . . you mean gynecologist. A geneologist is somebody who looks up people's background.

Jose: Wasn't my way a nicer way of putting it?

*   *   *

Sawbone Sillies

Doctor Stinehart examined Roderick and then asked, "Have you been living a normal life?"

"Yes, doctor," replied the patient.

"Well, you'll have to cut it out for a while."

* * *

"That's enough out of you," said the surgeon as he sewed up his patient.

9

At a recent Georgia medical convention a group of Atlanta physicians were having lunch. One said to the man beside him, "I operated on that wealthy Mrs. Simpson yesterday. Appendectomy, you know."

"Now the appendix, eh?" said his fellow surgeon. "Have you ever discovered what her real trouble is?"

* * *

Louis Wildman, Florida's video mogul, makes merry with this mouthful of mirth:

In Delaware, Dr. Kasten's practice began to decrease. He consulted Dr. Millard, a friend, who agreed to spend a few days in the office and observe his methods.

After an hour the other physician had the answer. "Kasten, when writing out a prescription, you've got to stop humming, 'Nearer My God To Thee!' "

* * *

"Oh, doctor, I'm so nervous! This is my first operation."

"I know just how you feel. You're my first patient!"

* * *

Never trust a doctor who tells you you're dead. Get a second opinion.

* * *

Doctor: Your pulse is as steady as a clock.
Patient: You've got your hand on my wrist-
watch.

* * *

"For leprosy, go to Devil's Island."
"Is that good for it, Doctor?"
"That's where I got mine."

* * *

"Did you hear about Frank's son?"
"No, what happened?"
"He was thrown out of medical school
for performing an illegal operation."
"Really? What?"
"He opened his teacher's head with a
hatchet."

* * *

"Doctor, my husband limps because
his right leg is shorter than his left. What
would you do in his case?"
"Probably limp."

Martin Sinaisky, California's consummate obstetrician, cracks up patients with this corker:

The best known surgeon in the world was invited to Cedars of Lebanon hospital in Los Angeles to perform an intricate operation. Every off-duty intern gathered in the gallery to watch.

At the most critical moment another doctor tapped the famous surgeon on the shoulder and said, "May I cut in?"

Doctor Strickland, returning from an emergency call, stopped in a Detroit diner. While studying the various selections, he looked up to see his waitress, Miss Kocynski, scratching her rear end. "You got hemorrhoids?" asked the doctor.

"Sorry, no special orders," said the girl. "Just what's on the menu."

* * *

Wyoming homemaker Jo Bonnett tells about Perry, an elderly man who visited a doctor for a physical. After the examination the doctor announced, "You're as fit as a fiddle. You'll live to be eighty."

"But, I am eighty!" said Perry.

"See, what did I tell you?" said the M.D.

* * *

MEDICAL ADVICE #2

Never trust a doctor who attaches a pacemaker to your heart with Crazy Glue.

* * *

Harrison had a leak in his bathroom plumbing, and even though it was 3:00 A.M., he decided to phone his plumber.

"My God, Doc!" he cried. "What a time to wake a guy."

"Well," said the doctor, "you've never hesitated to wake me in the middle of the night with a medical problem. This is a plumbing emergency."

"Okay, what's wrong?" said the plumber.

The doctor described the leak.

"Here's what you do," said the plumber. "Take two aspirin and drop them down the pipe. If the problem hasn't cleared up by morning, phone me at the office."

* * *

MEDICAL ADVICE #3

Never trust a doctor who uses a tongue depressor that tastes like Baskin & Robbins' flavor of the month.

* * *

A myopic tree surgeon named Lee
Trapped an agile young wench in a tree.
Jeered she, "Shift your whopper,
You careless limb-lopper!
That's a moss-covered knothole—not me!"

* * *

Tom Huffman, the top RCA TV technician, tells this tail-wagger:

Stuart had a sore throat and was ushered into Dr. Odell's office.

"I'm having trouble with my throat," he said.

"Go into my examining room and get undressed," said the doctor. "I'll be right with you."

Stuart stripped to his skin and sat down to wait. He noticed another man in the room completely naked but holding a large package.

"What's with this doctor?" asked Stuart. "I got trouble with my throat and he makes me take off all my clothes!"

"That's nothing," was the reply. "I came here to deliver a package!"

Hamilton, a young doctor, returned to his home town and met Hoskins, the old family physician.

"I suppose you intend to specialize," said Hoskins.

"Oh, yes," replied the youth, "diseases of the nose. The ears and throat are too complicated to be combined with the nose for purposes of study and treatment."

"Which nostril are you concentrating on?" quipped the old M.D.

* * *

Baker had a sore thumb and went to Doctor Manning. After an examination the M.D. said, "Go home and soak it in cold water."

Baker was sitting at home with his thumb in cold water when his wife walked in. "What're you doin'?" she asked.

"I hurt my thumb this morning, and the doctor told me to soak it in cold water."

"Boy, are you dumb," sneered Mrs. Baker. "The best thing to use is hot water."

Baker soaked his thumb in hot water and in three days it was healed. That afternoon he met Doctor Manning at the gas station. "Say," said Baker, "when I hurt my thumb and came to your office you told me to soak it in cold water. My wife told me to soak it in hot water and it got better."

"I'm sorry," said the doctor. "My wife says cold water!"

18

*Never trust a doctor who has a nurse
with a "PROPERTY OF HELL'S ANGELS"
tattoo.*

* * *

Sidney Kreps, the magnetic Manhattan
internist, brightens patients with this dash of
monkeyshines:

Dr. Irving Finkelstein, the great Israeli
surgeon, had been touring America to dem-
onstrate a brilliant appendectomy technique
that left no scar.

In Hollywood a film producer needed
his appendix removed. His wedding was in
2 weeks, so he insisted Dr. Finkelstein perform the operation.

When the movie mogul came out of
the ether, he found his lower body swathed
in bandages. "Nurse," he screamed, "there
ain't supposed to be a scar. What the hell
are all these bandages?"

"Well," she replied, "Dr. Finkelstein
performed the operation in a large amphi-
theater with over a hundred surgeons watching.
When he finished, they gave him a standing
ovation. He took several bows but they refused to stop applauding. Dr. Finkelstein
got so carried away that for an encore he
circumcised you."

Bruce Merrin, the popular Hollywood publicist, contributed this parable of pleasure:

Doctor Tilman just got married. He and his bride were spending their honeymoon in Meadow Park, high up in the Colorado mountains.

Overcome by the beauty of the scene, the bride turned to her new husband and said, "Oh, darling, aren't those clouds a fantasy of color?"

"Yes," said the doctor. "That one over there is particularly nice. It's the exact color of a cirrhotic liver."

Dr. Lamb had just completed the operation and was washing up. He was joined by one of the young interns, who inquired, "How did Mrs. Fuller's appendectomy go?"

"Appendectomy?" shrieked the surgeon, "I thought it was an autopsy!"

* * *

MEDICAL ADVICE #5

Never trust a doctor who stores his hypodermic needles on a dartboard.

* * *

That brilliant young Doctor Levine,
Fooled around with a brand new vaccine,
    Gave himself an injection,
    And it sure killed infection,
But it also grew hair on his spleen.

* * *

"My doctor has the flu."
"Too bad."
"Yeah, he's getting a taste of his own medicine."

* * *

What are the first two things a doctor learns at medical school?

Write your prescription illegibly and your bills clearly.

* * *

SIGN IN GYNECOLOGIST'S OFFICE

Standing Womb Only

* * *

Millbank and Furman were chatting in the hospital cafeteria.

"I operated on MacFarland last week," said Millbank.

"What for?" asked Furman.

"Six hundred dollars."

"What did he have?"

"Six hundred dollars."

* * *

Hedrick and Douglas, two doctors, were conversing in front of the hospital when two really attractive blondes came towards them.

"Here comes my wife and my girl-friend," said Hedrick.

"That's odd," said Douglas. "I was just gonna say the same thing to you."

* * *

23

Dave Scanlin, the sunny Sunset Books Western Sales Director, savors this smile-cracker:

Dr. Stranton died and arrived at the Pearly Gates. While trying to get through, he was stopped by St. Peter. "Now hold on," said the M.D. "I'll have you know I was the biggest heart specialist in Chicago. You've got to let me in."

"Sorry," said St. Peter. "You have to go to the rear of the line and wait your turn."

Dr. Stranton moved to the back of the queue and stood there. Suddenly, he spotted a man dressed in a green operating outfit, wearing a surgical mask and a stethoscope, walk past him and then straight through the Pearly Gates.

Stranton rushed up to St. Peter and shouted, "What's the meaning of this? I was here before that man. How dare you let him in?"

"Sorry," explained St. Peter. "That's God. You see, he thinks he's a doctor."

Did you hear about the obstetrician who put himself through medical school by working in the Post Office?

Now it takes him three months to deliver a baby.

* * *

Adamson telephoned Doctor Draper, the family physician, and said he was afraid his teenage son had come down with V.D.

"He says he hasn't had sex with anyone but the maid," offered Adamson, "so it has to be her."

"Don't worry," said Dr. Draper. "These things happen."

"I know, doctor," said the father, "but I have to admit that I've been to bed with her myself. And I seem to have the same symptoms."

"That's unfortunate."

"Not only that—I think I've passed them on to my wife."

"Oh Christ," moaned the medico. "That means we all have it."

* * *

A doctor fell in a deep well
    And broke his collar-bone.
The moral: Doctor, mind the sick
    And leave the well alone.

* * *

Hennesy stuttered badly. After many years of suffering his wife said, "Please see a doctor. You're driving me crazy."

Hennesy agreed. When the physician finished his examination, he said, "I've found the problem. It's your penis. It's the longest one I've ever seen. It's so heavy that it's pulling on your vocal cords and that's what's causing you to stutter."

"B-b-but, w-w-what c-c-can you d-do t-to help m-m-me?"

"I'll have to cut part of your pecker off."

After the operation, Hennesy talked perfectly. But Mrs. Hennesy missed her husband's enormous organ and insisted he get it put back on. Hennesy returned to the doctor and said, "I don't care if I stutter. I'd rather have my manhood back."

The doctor said, "S-s-sorry, it's t-t-too l-l-late now!"

* * *

Doctor Kulik picked up his phone. It was Miss Thompson, a pretty patient.

"Doctor," she said sweetly, "would you look around your office and see if I left my panties there this morning?"

The physician searched the room and then said, "I'm sorry, your panties aren't here!"

"Oh, gosh!" exclaimed Miss Thompson. "I must've left them at the dentist's!"

Toothpuller Titters

Fred and Gary were having lunch.

"I gotta leave in a few minutes," said Fred. "I got a terrible toothache, and I'm going to the dentist and have it out."

"That's dumb," said Gary. "Yesterday I had a toothache, too. I went home; my wife made love to me, and the pain left me like that. Why don't you try it?"

"That's a great idea. Call up your wife and tell her I'll be right over."

* * *

Why did the dentist's wife shoot him? She found out he was filling the wrong cavities.

There was a young lady named Twilling
Who went to her dentist for drilling.
Because of depravity,
He filled the wrong cavity,
And now Twilling's nursing her fill-
ing.

* * *

Robert Abeloff, Beverly Hills' dentist
to the stars, beams over this bubbler:
Higlemire and his wife entered the dentist's office.
"I want a tooth pulled," he said.
"We're in a big hurry, so let's not fool
around with gas or Novocain or any of that
stuff."
"You're a very brave man," remarked
the dentist. "Which tooth is it?"
"Show him your bad tooth, honey,"
said the man to his wife.

* * *

Satterfield sat in the office of Dr. Hobbs.
"I've got an emergency out at my house,
Doc," muttered Satterfield. "My son Steve
was kissing his girlfriend while his mother
and I were out this afternoon, and he got his
braces locked."
"No problem," said the dentist. "I
have to unlock teenagers' braces all the
time."
"From an I.U.D.?"

30

Bobby: Dad, that man wasn't a painless dentist like he advertised.

Dad: Why? Did he hurt you?

Bobby: No, but he yelled when I bit his thumb.

* * *

Did you hear about the guru who refused to let the dentist use Novocain to numb his mouth?

The guru said he wanted to transcend dental medication.

* * *

The jovial actor Lou Jacobi tells about the dentist who's such a bore, his patients ask for gas even when he's cleaning their teeth!

* * *

A dentist named Englebert Moss
Fell in love with the dainty Miss Ross
But he held in abhorrence
Her Christian name, Florence,
So he renamed her his Dental Floss.

* * *

"Okay, Doc, let's have it!"

"Well, your teeth are all right, but the gums will have to come out."

Chuck Mindlin, the majestic orthodontist, peppers patients with this mountain of merriment:

Barth went to Dr. Legget to get a cavity filled. He escorted Barth to the chair and gave him some Novocain. Legget returned a few moments later, told him to open his mouth wide, and then reached for his drill.

Suddenly the dentist stiffened and said to the man, "Mr. Barth, do you realize your hand is clutching my testicles?"

"Certainly, Doctor," he replied. "We're not going to hurt each other, are we?"

Overton, sitting in the dentist's chair, shouted, "Hey, Doc, you haven't pulled the right tooth!"

"I know it," replied the D.D.S. "but I'm coming to it."

* * *

Dr. Holgate stopped at a cocktail lounge every evening on the way home for his special drink: a frozen almond daiquiri. This concoction was made with the standard ingredients plus some crushed almonds. All Dr. Holgate had to do was come through the door, and the bartender would toss the makings into the blender.

One evening, the bartender had the drink half-prepared when he discovered that the bar was out of almonds. He added crushed hickory nuts instead.

The dentist took one sip and asked the bartender, "Is this an almond daiquiri?"

"No," he replied. "It's a hickory daiquiri, Doc."

* * *

An attractive, though silly girl, Ruth,
Had a horror of telling the truth
    To her dentist she lied
    As his pliers he plied
So he cheerfully pulled the wrong tooth.

* * *

BIBLICAL BENEDICTION

*Be true to thy teeth, and they will not
be false to thee*

* * *

Di Angelo went into Dr. Gaffney's office and immediately requested that the nurse leave the room. The dentist sent her out. Then the patient unzipped his fly and took out his pecker.

"Listen," said Gaffney, "you're in the wrong place. I don't treat clap. Why don't you go to an M.D.?"

"No, you're the man I want to see," said Di Angelo. "There's a tooth embedded in it."

* * *

Did you hear about the fearless hunter in the jungles of Ceylon who was so anxious to bag a leopard that, in the excitement, his false teeth fell out?

Ever since the poor man has been searching for his bridge on the River Kwai.

* * *

Norman Krevoy, the prominent California oral surgeon, came up with this corker:

Dr. Rodecker had done extensive dental work for a world famous surrealist painter. The artist was very pleased with the results. In addition to paying his bill he said he would like to show his appreciation by presenting the dentist with one of his paintings.

A few weeks later a large canvas arrived. It was a painting of an enormous mouth. The mouth was wide open, surrounded by huge prominent teeth and in the center was a portrait of Dr. Rodecker.

The dentist's wife was flabbergasted when she saw the painting. "Good Lord!" she said: "Am I glad I didn't marry a proctologist!"

MEDICAL ADVICE #6

Never trust a dentist who mixes your
fillings from a recipe in a Betty Crocker
Cook Book

* * *

Dr. Lazarus completed his examination of the Texas oil millionaire's teeth and said, "You have no cavities!"

"Drill anyway," drawled the Texan. "Ah had mah horoscope read his mornin', and today's mah lucky day!"

* * *

"You've got a good dentist?"

"Oh, he's great. Every bridge he makes for you is guaranteed for the life of your gums."

* * *

It is easy enough to be happy
When life is a bright, rosy wreath
But the man worthwhile
Is the man who can smile
When the dentist is filling his teeth.

* * *

*   *   *

She had been putting it off for years.
Each of her six children pleaded and then
finally together they all insisted. Finally, old
Mrs. Kazinski had some dentures made.
Three days later she returned to Dr. Wallach's
office.

"You know those teeth you make for
me?" she asked. "They're no good. They
don't fit."

"That's not too unusual," replied the
dentist. "Let's check your bite and see what
the trouble is."

After performing several bite tests, Wallach announced, "As far as I can see they
fit fine!"

"I not talking about my mouth," said
the woman. "They don't fit in the glass."

*   *   *

Did you hear about the dentist who
went back to medical school to become a
gynecologist?

He wanted to get into bigger cavities.

*   *   *

39

Jon Sonneborn, the peerless Video Images prexy, pleases friends with this playful pearl:

McKenna sat in a Cleveland dentist's chair counting his money.

"Sir, you don't have to pay me in advance," said the doctor.

"I know that," said the Scotsman. "I was just counting my money before you gave me the gas."

41

O'Sullivan staggered out of the corner saloon and into Dr. Horn's office complaining about a toothache. Unfortunately, the Irishman was terribly squeamish about having the infected molar extracted. To bolster his morale Dr. Horn poured him a stiff shot of whiskey and then asked, "Ready now?"

"Not quite yet," said O'Sullivan, smacking his lips. Two more slugs of whiskey found him still reluctant, so the dentist let him finish the bottle.

"Now step into the chair," asked Horn. The Irishman began shadow boxing in the middle of the room. He swung wildly and then exclaimed, "I'd like to see the rascal who'd dare touch me teeth now."

* * *

Dentist: Stop making faces. I haven't even touched your tooth yet.
Thorson: I know you haven't, but you're standing on my foot!

* * *

At breakfast one morning Dr. Parker said to his wife, "Looks like old MacPherson isn't going to pay any attention to the bills I've sent him. I'm going up to his house and collect in person."

An hour later he was back, looking downhearted. "I can see by your face that he didn't pay you," said his wife.

"He not only didn't pay me," said the dentist. "He bit me with my own teeth."

* * *

MacGregor had a toothache and went to Dr. Friedman.

"What do you charge for extracting a tooth?" asked the Scotsman.

"Fifty dollars," replied the dentist.

"Fifty dollars for only twenty seconds' work?" exclaimed MacGregor.

"Well," replied the dentist, "if you want, I could extract it very slowly."

* * *

Brady complained to the doctor about a very unusual problem. Whenever he passed gas, it made a noise like a motorcycle. The physician ran a complete series of tests and could find nothing. "You'll just have to learn to live with it," said the M.D.

The following week Brady went to the dentist for a check-up. "You've got a nasty looking abcess there," said the dentist, "but I can clear that up. Of course, this will also cure those motorcycle noises."

"How could you possibly know about that?" asked Brady, surprised.

"It's quite simple, really. Abcess makes the fart go Honda."

There was an old man named McLeath
Who sat on his own false teeth.
    Said he with a cry,
    "I should use my eye.
"Here I've bitten myself underneath."

* * *

HELP WANTED

Dentist, part or pull time

* * *

"Has your tooth stopped aching?"
"I don't know. My dentist kept it."

* * *

Dr. Young was halfway through some bridgework on a pretty blonde when his machine stopped running. "I'm afraid I'm out of gas," he said.

"I knew it!" she exclaimed, jumping out of the chair. "All you guys try to pull the same routine!"

* * *

A reporter interviewed Linda Lovelace's dentist and extracted this quote from him:

"I've never come across such teeth!"

A two-toothed old man of Arbroath
Gave vent to a terrible oath.
> When one tooth chanced to ache,
> By an awful mistake,
The dentist extracted them both.

* * *

Dr. Cory was having an affair with one of his patients. One day she was sitting in the dentist's chair and he said, "Sweetheart, we can't see each other any more. You're down to your last tooth."

* * *

"You like your new dentist?"
"I think he might be into S & M. He's got bull whips made from dental floss hanging in his office."

* * *

TOOTHY TUNE

*She was only the dentist's daughter,
but she ran around with the worst
set in town.*

Did you hear about the dentist who married a manicurist?

They've been fighting tooth and nail ever since.

* * *

Dr. Margolis had a very nervous patient in Mrs. Lipsky. She panicked the moment she sat in his chair and clamped her mouth so tightly that he couldn't pry it open.

One morning Margolis had his nurse sneak up behind her, and when he was ready to drill, the nurse jabbed Mrs. Lipsky in the rear with a stick pin. She opened her mouth to holler, and Margolis was able to finish his work.

When it was all over the dentist said, "Now that wasn't so bad after all, was it?"

"No," she admitted, "but I didn't expect to feel the pain so far down!"

* * *

Shrinker Shenanigans

Thornton began his first session with the psychiatrist.

"I occasionally suffer from complete loss of memory," said the patient. "What do you advise?"

"That you always pay me in advance."

Dr. Davies and Dr. Hummel met at a dinner party and began discussing their cases.

"One of my patients has a split personality," said Davies.

"That's not a very unusual case," replied Hummel.

"This one is," said the first shrink. "They both pay."

* * *

Did you hear about the psychiatrist who had a sectional couch for treating split personalities?

* * *

Platt had a terrible fear of thunder. He just couldn't stand to hear it. Finally, in desperation, he went to an eminent psychiatrist.

"That's ridiculous!" said the crazy-doctor, "Thunder is a natural phenomenon, and nothing to be afraid of. Whenever you hear thunder, do just what I do: Put your head under the pillow and it will go away."

* * *

Dr. Ward: Why do you hate your sister?
Jansen: I don't have a sister.
Dr. Ward: If you expect me to help you, you've got to cooperate.

48

EX-PSYCHIATRIST

Shrunk

* * *

"There's nothing wrong with you," said Dr. Sinclair to his patient. "Why, you're just as sane as I am!"

The patient began brushing himself and exclaimed, "But what about these butter-flies? They're all over me!"

"For God's sake," cried the doctor. "Don't brush them off on me!"

* * *

Dr. Alden and Dr. Peake were compar-ing cases at a medical convention.

"What was your toughest case?" asked Alden.

"This man suffering from delusions of grandeur," replied Peake. "For years, he had been telling everyone that he was wait-ing for a letter stating that he would inherit a diamond mine in South Africa and an oil field in Hawaii."

"What happened?"

"Every day for five years I struggled through long sessions with him and finally, just when he was completely cured, the damn letter arrived!"

"I've got good news for you, Mr. Clary," said the shrink.

"What's that?" said the patient.

"How long have I been treating you for kleptomania?"

"About two years."

"I'm happy to say you're cured. You won't be shoplifting any more."

"Are you sure, Doctor?"

"Of course. Just to prove it to you, stop off at Macy's and walk all through the store. You'll see, you are no longer a kleptomaniac."

"Thanks a lot, Doc."

"But listen, if you have a relapse, I could use a 9-inch color TV."

* * *

What's the difference between a psychologist and a psychiatrist?

A psychologist is a blind man in a pitch dark basement looking for a black cat.

A psychiatrist is a blind man in a pitch dark basement looking for a black cat that isn't there.

* * *

Dr. Toni Grant, the glamorous Los Angles radio star, gets giggles with this goofy gag:

Koppel, prone on the couch, began talking to the head shrinker.

"I see my brother," said Koppel, "he is walking out in a courtyard. He gets to a wooden structure and goes up 13 steps. There are lots of people standing around. They're putting a blindfold over his eyes. Doctor, what does it mean?"

"Well," said the psychiatrist, "if they aren't playing blindman's bluff, he's in real trouble."

* * *

Psychiatrist to patient: You're quite right. A man is following you constantly. He's trying to collect the $600 you owe me.

* * *

Did you hear about the psychiatrist who gave his son a set of mental blocks for Christmas?

* * *

Mike Sackett, the scholarly Ohio hockey star, gets howls with this humdinger:

Tuft was lying on Dr. Polk's couch when suddenly he leaped up and said, "Doctor, I've got a compulsion to knock over that lamp!"

"Go ahead!" said the shrink.

And he did. Then Tuft said, "I feel I gotta tear down all the picture frames from the wall!"

"Go ahead," said Polk, "do anything you feel you need to!"

So he did.

Tuft walked over to the office window, which was twenty floors up, and said, "Doctor, I've got an urge—I want to jump out!"

"If that'll make you happy, give in to the urge!" said the shrink.

Tuft opened the window and jumped.

The doctor ran to the window and shouted, "Yippee!"

* * *

MAD MONEY

A psychiatrist's fee

* * *

Dr. Reddington, aged 37, and Dr. Woolford, who was in his seventies, occupied offices in the same building. At the end of a hot August day, the two psychoanalysts rode on the elevator together.

Reddington was completely done in, and noted with some irritation that his older colleague looked as fresh as a Spring morning.

"I don't understand how you can look so spry after listening to babbling patients from morning till night," said the younger man.

The older analyst replied, "Who listens?"

* * *

Did you hear about the Irish psychiatrist who uses a Murphy bed instead of a couch?

* * *

* * *

Gary complained to the psychiatrist about his continuing problem with girls.

"I've tried everything," he said. "Cologne, sexy toothpaste, the right deodorant. I still can't find sexual relief."

"Have you ever tried auto-eroticism?" asked the shrink.

"Hell, no," answered Gary. "I jerk off at home."

* * *

Dr. Shaw brought the young woman into his office and gestured toward the couch.

"Do you mind if I stand?" she asked. "I just got back from my honeymoon."

* * *

A beautiful chorus girl walked into the psychiatrist's office. The moment she closed the door, the doctor pulled her down on the couch, ripped off her clothes and attacked her.

Ten minutes later he got up and said, "Well, that takes care of my problem. Now what's yours?"

* * *

Melvin Schlemenson, the super story-telling surgeon, puts patients in stitches with this spirit-lifter:

Betty, a beautiful Broadway showgirl, revealed to Dr. Dailey that her problem was liquor.

"Do you drink much?" asked the psychiatrist.

"No, but if I just have one drink, I want to make love to whomever I am with at that moment."

"Well," said the doctor, "why don't I fix us each a martini, then you and I can relax and discuss this compulsion of yours!"

* * *

Neal consulted a psychiatrist about his nymphomaniac girlfriend. "Doctor," he stammered, "she has the weirdest, bizarre sexual desires. She craves sex morning, noon, and . . ."

"That's enough," interrupted the shrink. "Does she have a friend?"

* * *

After nearly a year of three visits a week to the analyst she could no longer control her desire. Right in the middle of her session, Mrs. Jardine exclaimed, "Dr. Shaw, I'm crazy about you. Please kiss me!"

"No," replied the shrink. "That would be contrary to the ethics of my profession. Now go on as before."

"Well," continued the patient. "I'm always fighting with my husband about sex. . . . I'm sorry, Doctor, but what harm would it be if you kissed me just once?"

"That's impossible!" said the doctor. "In fact, I shouldn't even be lying on this couch with you!"

* * *

NEUROTIC—builds castles in the air
PSYCHOTIC—lives in the castles
PSYCHIATRIST—collects the rent from both

Penelope, a pretty stewardess, lay on Dr. Rolland's couch. Holding up a square, the head shrinker instructed, "Look at this and tell me the first thing that comes into your mind."

"A penis!" said Penelope.

He produced a circle, "What are you thinking of now?" he asked.

"A penis!" she replied.

Waving a triangle, he demanded, "And now?"

"A penis!"

The shrink said, "It appears you have a thing called penis envy."

"Me?" snapped the girl. "You're the one who's sitting there with his fly wide open!"

* * *

"My psychiatrist is booked solid every day."

"How come?"

"It's since he covered the ceiling around his couch with *Gallery Magazine* centerfolds."

* * *

Rosanne was on the young psychiatrist's couch. "Oh, doctor," she cried, "I'm so worried. I think I'm a nymphomaniac."

The analyst zipped down his fly and said, "I think I've got just the thing for you."

* * *

Busy psychiatrist to nurse: "All right, send in that nymphomaniac and take the rest of the day off."

* * *

Did you hear about the psychiatrist who had his office decorated with new furniture made of overwrought iron?

* * *

60

* * *

Judith, a lovely Manhattan model, had poured her heart out to Dr. Sumner. "Maybe if my body was less attractive," she concluded. "I wouldn't have so much trouble with men."

"You are a very sick young lady," said the shrink. "I don't want you to work this afternoon. Go home, get undressed, and get into bed. Drink about a third of this bottle of medicine. It will make you drowsy. I don't want you to answer your phone or let anybody into your apartment until you hear three short knocks. . . ."

* * *

Mrs. Page, the oversexed young wife of a movie mogul, went to a psychiatrist who specialized in sexual problems.

Two hours later she phoned her husband on location in Canada. "Darling, guess what," she cooed. "I think I finally found a doctor to lick my problems."

* * *

* * *

Phoebe, an attractive secretary, seated herself at the young psychologist's desk. "What seems to be the trouble?" he asked.

"Well," she answered, turning red, "I think I'm a nymphomaniac."

"I can probably help you," said the doctor, "but I must tell you that my fee is fifty dollars an hour."

"That's not bad," said Phoebe. "How much for all night?"

* * *

Near the end of their first session, the psychiatrist asked his pretty patient, "Do you think you might be a nymphomaniac?"

"Certainly not!" she exclaimed. "I don't even like it more than seven or eight times a day."

* * *

The macho Hollywood actor was being analyzed.

"Tell me," asked the psychoanalyst, "Do you ever cheat on your wife?"

"Who else?"

* * *

*   *   *

Mrs. Collins sat nervously before the psychiatrist and said, "I caught my son and the little girl next door examining each other with their pants down."

"That's not so unusual," said the doctor. "Children like to compare things. I wouldn't get upset."

"I'm already upset," said the woman, "and so is my son's wife."

*   *   *

Camila had come to see Dr. Hardy. When the shrink began using sexual terms, she interrupted, "Wait, what is a phallic symbol?"

"A phallic symbol," explained Hardy, "represents the phallus."

"What's a phallus?" asked Camila.

"Well," said the analyst, "the best way to explain it is to show you." He stood up, unzipped his fly and took out his pecker.

"This is a phallus."

"Oh," said the girl. "It's just like a prick, only smaller."

*   *   *

Jonah Perlmutter, the brilliant Beverly Hills analyst, beams broadly at this bit of burlesque:

Reynolds, just back from hunting wild game in Africa, sat in Dr. Fletcher's office. "Look, Doc," said Reynolds, "I don't want to go through analysis, but I'll pay you $500 to answer two questions."

"That's rather unusual," said the shrink, "but I'll go along with it."

"Is it possible," asked the hunter, "for a man to be in love with an elephant?"

"Definitely impossible," said the psychiatrist. "I've never heard of it. Not in all the annals of psychiatry. The whole idea is ridiculous. What's your second question?"

Reynolds asked, "Do you know anyone who wants to buy a very large engagement ring?"

Lenore listened intently as the shrink said, "Tell me about your daylight fantasies. Do you do housework in the nude? Do you wonder how the brush of a feather duster feels against naked nipples? Have you thought of relieving your lustful instincts with the end of a broom handle?"

"Shame on you, Doctor," said the blonde. "You've been peeking through my kitchen window!"

*   *   *

Dr. Deming, a frumpy middle-aged woman psychiatrist, did volunteer work at the State Penitentiary. Her most difficult patient was a handsome weight-lifter who day after day spoke nothing but nonsense.

Finally she said, "Young man, why can't you make at least one definite statement?"

"Okay," said the jailbird. "I want to rip off your panty hose and screw you to death."

"Good," said the lady shrink. "At last you're making sense."

*   *   *

Loony Bin Levity

layton was visiting

his brother at the asylum. "Is there anything I can get you?" he asked.

"Yes," replied his brother, "I'd like a watch that tells time."

"Doesn't your watch tell time?"

"No," said the inmate. "I have to look at it."

Burgess and Newton, two inmates, were sitting on the grass.

"I've made up my mind," said Burgess. "Tomorrow I order my legions to invade England. History will say that Julius Caesar was the greatest general who ever lived.

"England, eh?" said Newton, "Well, Julius, if I were you . . . and, incidentally, I am . . ."

The Governor was being shown around the state asylum by the chief administrator. They came upon an inmate whose lips would move for a moment, and then he would laugh hilariously.

The nut did this several times, and then suddenly he turned silent.

"What's that man doing?" asked the Governor.

"He's telling himself jokes," replied the administrator.

"I notice he didn't laugh at the last one he told," said the Governor. "How do you explain that?"

"Oh," said the chief. "He heard that one before."

All day long Fleming pushed a wheelbarrow around the asylum grounds upside down.

Finally, an attendant said to him: "That's no way to push a wheelbarrow. Turn it right side up when you push it."

"I did at first," said Fleming. "But they kept putting bricks in it."

* * *

A congressman got stuck in a storm while visiting a rural mental institution. He tried for hours to get a long distance call through but was unsuccessful.

In desperation he shouted angrily at the operator, "Young lady, do you know who I am?"

"No, sir," she replied, "but I know *where* you are."

* * *

Russell, a loony, was playing solitaire. Drake, another nut, was watching. Suddenly Drake cried, "Hold it! I just saw you cheating yourself."

"Shhh!" whispered Russell, "don't tell anybody, but I've been cheating myself at solitaire for years."

"Really," said his pal. "Don't you ever catch yourself?"

"Naw," said the first loon. "I'm too clever."

Murray Davis, the well-known West Coast home builder, came up with this cuckoo:

Copeland, a contractor, while visiting an asylum, found inmate Blake building a new outer wall. Up on a ladder, Blake was laying bricks as skillfully as a pro.

"Say," shouted Copeland, "how're you getting along in this place?"

"Real good," replied the bricklayer. "The doc says I'll be leaving soon."

"How'd you like to come and work for me?" asked the contractor.

"Okay," said the inmate.

"Listen," said Copeland, "I'll be back Monday, and I'll try to fix it so you can get out even sooner."

"Wonderful," said Blake.

Just then a brick came flying down, hit Copeland in the head and knocked him to the ground.

"Hey," called the nut. "You won't forget Monday, will you?"

* * *

A senator was speaking in a mental institution. During the talk, an inmate called out, "Lousy." Later, he shouted a little louder: "Lousy." Then he got really loud: "Lousy!"

The senator said to the superintendent, "Can't you keep that man quiet? This is very annoying."

"Are you kidding?" he said. "It's the first intelligent word he's spoken in ten years!"

* * *

Salisbury sat on a bench in the asylum grounds enjoying the sun, his hands clasped together. Every now and then he would peek in between his hands.

Babcock, another goony loon, joined him and asked, "What you got there?"

"Guess!" said Salisbury.

"Butterfly?" guessed his pal.

The screwball took a careful peek. "Nope."

"Hummingbird?" asked Babcock.

Salisbury took another look. "Nope."

"An elephant, maybe?"

The screwball took another long look.

"All right," he said. "But what color?"

* * *

* * *

Meyler was visiting the funny farm and found an inmate rocking back and forth in a chair cooing, "Gloria . . . Gloria . . . !"

"What's wrong with this man?" Meyler asked the attendant.

"Well," he explained, "Gloria was the woman who jilted him."

Meyler continued the tour and came to a padded cell, where an inmate was batting his head against the wall and crying "Gloria, Gloria!"

"Why is *he* crying 'Gloria'?" asked the visitor.

"He's the guy Gloria married," said the attendant.

* * *

Dr. Crane looked at the inmate sitting beside his desk and announced, "I've got good news for you, Mr. Ryder. After reviewing your case, I've concluded that you're cured."

"That's terrible," answered Ryder. "Two years ago, I was Teddy Roosevelt. Today, I'm a nobody!"

* * *

Golden, the new mental institution supervisor, stopped one of the inmates and asked him his name.

"Abraham Lincoln," said the man.

A few hours later, on returning, Golden passed the nut again. "What did you say your name was?" he asked.

"George Washington," said the guy.

"Funny," said the supervisor, "I could've sworn you told me your name was Abraham Lincoln."

"That," said the loony, "was by my first wife."

* * *

Hamlin had a flat tire in front of an asylum. As he took the wheel off, the bolts that held the wheel on rolled down into the sewer.

An inmate looking through the fence observed the incident. "Listen," he suggested, "just take one bolt from the other three wheels to hold the fourth wheel in place until you can get to the gas station."

"Thanks a lot," said Hamlin. "I don't know why you are in that place."

"I'm here for being crazy, not for being stupid."

* * *

Brucker, an asylum inmate, complained about a cat in his stomach. "He's jumping around and clawing me apart," said the loony.

One day Brucker got an appendicitis attack, and the surgeon decided to take advantage of the operation. He sent for a black cat. When the inmate came out of the ether the doctor held up the animal and said, "You're okay now. Look what we got."

"No, no," shouted the inmate. "You've got the wrong cat. The one I swallowed was gray."

* * *

A big Cadillac pulled up in front of a nuthouse and out stepped Coberly, a distinguished, grey-haired banker. He approached the gate attendant and said, "Is this an asylum for the insane?"

"Yes, sir," said the gateman.

"Do they take inmates who would be willing to commit themselves?"

"I don't know. Why?"

"I just got hold of a package of my old love letters and . . ."

* * *

Highland Park's handsome Hank Ralson sent in this snappy snicker:

A senator was visiting his state's mental institution. As he strolled through the grounds he came upon an unusual sight. A patient sitting on a bench was holding a fish pole and line over a large pail of water.

"What are you fishing for?" asked the senator.

"Suckers," said the loon.

"Catch any?" asked the politician.

"You're the eighth!"

EiGHT!!!

A guard from a psychiatric hospital rushed up to Beggs, a farmer on the road, and said, "I'm looking for an escaped lunatic. Did he pass this way?"

"What'd he look like?" asked Farmer Beggs.

"He's short and thin," said the guard, "and he weighs about 400 pounds."

"How in the devil can a man be short and thin and weigh 400 pounds?" asked the farmer.

"Well," said the guard. "I told you he was crazy."

* * *

Castro came to inspect a Cuban insane asylum. The inmates were assembled in the courtyard. According to instructions, they shouted: "Long live our beloved leader, the great Castro!"

A secret policemen noticed that one man did not pledge allegiance and grabbed him immediately.

"Why did you not greet our beloved Comrade Castro?" asked the agent.

"Because," said the man, "I'm not insane. I'm the janitor."

* * *

Inmate Ingram was strolling down the asylum hallway with one hand cupped over the other. Dr. Whitman, the psychiatrist, spotted him and asked, "What have you got in your hands!"

"A tomato worm," he said. "I'm going to get ten pounds of tomatoes."

Twenty minutes later Ingram returned to the asylum carrying a bushel of tomatoes.

The next afternoon Dr. Whitman caught the patient walking down the hallway again with his hands cupped.

"Now what do you have?" asked the psychiatrist.

"A horsefly. And I'm going out to find myself a horse."

An hour later, the lunatic returned leading a beautiful Arabian pony.

The next day, Dr. Whitman once again found Ingram coming down the hallway with hands cupped together.

"And what have you got this time?" he asked.

"A ladybug."

"Okay," said the shrink, "I'll go with you."

* * *

Nursing Nifties

Watkins telephoned the doctor for an appointment. The nurse said she could schedule him in two weeks.

"In two weeks I could be dead!" moaned Watkins.

"In that case," answered the nurse, "you can cancel the appointment!"

* * *

Claire, a young student nurse, went for her first driving test and flunked it. On her second try, Claire was so nervous she went right through a red light.

The officer said to her, "Doesn't a red light mean anything to you?"

"Of course. It means someone's ringing for a bedpan!"

* * *

The lecturer on physiology addressed the student nurses.

"Today, girls, we will take up the heart, lung, liver and kidneys."

"Another organ recital," whispered one nurse to the other.

* * *

"Nurse, that champagne glass I sat on—how can you be certain the doctor will get all the pieces out?"

"Simple. We'll reconstruct the glass."

* * *

Lockward was visiting a cousin in the hospital. He noticed that the nurses were all wearing pins on their uniforms. When he looked closer, Lockwad saw the pins were shaped like apples.

"Excuse me," he said to one of the girls. "Did you all graduate from the same nursing school?"

"Oh, no," answered the pretty young nurse. "We wear them to keep the doctors away!"

* * *

* * *

The supervisor was giving her final lecture to the nurses about to receive their caps.

"Remember, girls, cheerfulness is your chief stock in trade. What is the opposite of sorrow, Miss Snyder?"

"Joy."

"Exactly. And you, Miss Hart, what is the opposite of misery?"

"Happiness."

"Good. And now, Miss Frazer what is the opposite of woe?"

"Eh . . . Giddyup," she said.

* * *

NURSE

A panhandler

* * *

Mrs. Harker arrived at the doctor's office and grabbed his nurse, Miss Umbrowski.

"I would have been here sooner, but I have sitter trouble."

"Sitter trouble?" said the nurse. "You must be in the wrong office. Doctor is an eye specialist. You want a proctologist."

* * *

* * *

Johnny: Mama, I didn't know you could take a nurse apart.
Mother: What made you think you could?
Johnny: I heard Daddy say that last night he screwed the ass off a nurse.

* * *

Butler sat in the doctor's office and listed his complaints to the nurse: "I've got a bad case of arthritis, there's a buzzing in my ears, my ankle is sprained, I see spots in front of my eyes, and I've thrown my thumb out of joint."

"Wow!" exclaimed the nurse. "You must be real healthy to stand all that pain."

* * *

Did you hear about the Puerto Rican nurse who told the surgeon, "You asked for a local anesthetic, doctor, but the label on this bottle says it was made in Rochester."

* * *

The senior nursing instructor looked at Nurse Garcia. ''Why are you staring at your tummy?''

''I been putting on weight,'' answered the girl, ''and the supervisor said I should watch my stomach.''

* * *

Belmont had an unusually deep and husky voice. He appealed to Doctor Drake to castrate him, as his voice was a social nuisance.

The M.D. performed the operation, and two months later Belmont returned to complain of his new falsetto voice. Doctor Drake agreed to graft the testicles back, and began searching through his cabinets for them.

''Oh, Nurse,'' he called, ''did you see a little bottle sitting on this shelf the other day?''

The nurse replied in a deep, baritone voice, ''You mean the one with those two olives in it?''

* * *

Miss Simmons was a fantastically stacked lady in white. One evening she was walking down the hospital corridor, her uniform askew and part of her bosom showing, when she encountered the supervisor. The supervisor froze in shocked amazement. She then reprimanded Miss Simmons for her improper dress and shameful display of her body.

Straightening her clothes the young nurse blurted, "I'm really sorry, but you know those damned interns never put anything back when they're through with it!"

Crandall, feeling sick, had arrived when the doctor was out of the office. Ellen, his beautiful redheaded nurse, said to him, "Maybe I can help. Take off all your clothes in the examination room."

Five minutes later, she placed her hand on Crandall's throat and said, "Say thirty-three very slowly."

"Thirrrty thr-r-r-ee—ee!" repeated Crandall.

The voluptuous lady in white placed her hand on his heart and said, "Say thirty-three!"

"Thir-r-rty thr-r-r-ee!"

Ellen placed her on Crandall's stomach and again requested, "Say thirty-three."

He did it.

Now the nurse gently took hold of Crandall's genitals in her soft fingers. "Say thirty-three slowly!"

"One . . . two . . . three . . . four . . . ."

* * *

Nurse (to doctor): Every time I lean over to take Mr. Hayworth's heartbeat it increases. Something's wrong.

Doctor: Nothing's wrong. Just keep the top of your blouse buttoned.

* * *

Metcalf's mouth had been injured in an automobile accident, and to save it the emergency room intern grafted a piece of a nurse's labia to Metcalf's lip. A year later he met the doctor again and told him, "The scar's fine, but every time I get an erection my lip quivers."

* * *

Boyer dashed to the hospital to visit his spouse and newborn baby. At the door to his wife's room, he met a pretty nurse carrying a darling little baby swathed in cloth. Boyer ran his hand under the cloth and said to the nurse, "Isn't little Edward a handsome devil?"

"This one isn't yours," said the nurse. "This child's name is Peggy, and please let go of my finger."

* * *

PRACTICAL NURSE

One who marries a rich, elderly patient

* * *

* * *

Nurses dislike working with an egotistical, inconsiderate physician, especially if he bosses them around constantly.

Marion, Sybil, Dora, and Nancy had been assigned to such a doctor and decided at long last to retaliate and teach him a lesson.

They each planned a separate surprise for him, and when all four plots had been hatched they met to discuss their revenge.

"I stuffed cotton in the bottom of his stethoscope," said Marion. "Will he be surprised when he examines his patients tomorrow morning!"

"He sure will," said Sybil. "I let the mercury out of all his thermometers, and painted them to read 108°."

Dora giggled, "I did better than that. I went through his desk and found his private box of contraceptives. I took a pin and punched holes in every one of them."

Nancy, the fourth nurse, fainted.

* * *

Did you hear about the pregnant nurse whose theme song was "Witch Doctor"?

* * *

BUMPER STICKER

Nurses are patient people

* * *

Dr. Fullerton delivered his 400th baby. In the wash-up room a thought occurred to him. "Miss Daly," he said to the head nurse, "is it love or pride that causes a woman to squeal at the sight of her newborn child?"

"Neither one," answered the nurse. "It's the shock of seeing something pulled out of her bigger than it was when it went in."

* * *

"They call that new blonde on the third floor *Appendix*."

"That's an unusual name."

"They call her *Appendix* because all the interns want to take her out."

* * *

"Let's wiggle through real slow and
listen to the circumcision stitches pop!"

* * *

A famous movie star who had been
linked romantically with every beauty in
Hollywood entered a Manhattan hospital for
a check-up. Every nurse in the institution
fawned over him.

Bonita, a beautifully proportioned nurse,
was at his side every time he stirred. When
he finally indicated that he'd like to be alone
for just a little while, she told him, "Now if
you want anything at all, you need only pull
this cord."

"Thank you, my dear," he smiled.
"What is the cord attached to?"

"Me," answered Bonita.

* * *

Pretty Nurse: Each time I take this
patient's pulse it gets
faster. Should I give him
a sedative?

Doctor: No. A blindfolu.

* * *

* * *

Did you hear about the nurse who was so pretty that when she took a male patient's temperature she automatically subtracted 10 degrees.

* * *

Netta and Arlene were sitting in the nurses' lounge. "I believe women make the best doctors," said Netta.

"You're so right!" said Arlene. "I've made three or four cute ones myself!"

* * *

"I've got a pal in the hospital."
"How's he doin'?"
"He took a turn for the nurse!"

* * *

"I'm in love with you," the hospital patient told his nurse. "I don't want to get well."

"You won't," said the nurse. "The doctor saw you kissing me, and he's in love with me too."

* * *
94

Terry Winnick, the witty Universal Studios Tour veep, wins friends with this tail wagger:

Miss Hanson just started with Dr. Nason and wanted to make a good impression on the patients who came to his office. One morning, Banning arrived for his first visit.

"What kind of a guy is this doctor?" he asked.

"Best in the city," replied the nurse.

"Is he the kind that cuts you open at the drop of a hat?"

"Not this doctor," said Miss Hanson. "He never operates unless it's really necessary. In fact, if he doesn't need the money, he won't lay a hand on you."

* * *

"Matthew's gonna be in the hospital for a long, long time."

"How do you know? Did you see the doctor?"

"No. The nurse."

* * *

Miss Estrada, the new nurse, made lots of mistakes with the hypodermic needle, rectal thermometer and bedpan, but the young girl was determined to excel in her profession.

One afternoon, the doctor in charge of the ward was shocked to see one of his patients running down the hall in his white hospital robe howling at the top of his lungs. The nurse was chasing after him carrying a basin of steaming water.

"No! No! Miss Estrada!" exclaimed the doctor, "I told you to prick his boil!"

Miss Carmela, the student nurse, tucked in the bedclothes of a hospital patient.

"When the doctor comes on his rounds this morning," she said, "I want you to smile and look happy."

"I don't want to smile," said the patient. "I don't feel happy. I feel horrible."

"Try for the doctor's sake," said Miss Carmela. "It'd cheer him up. I happen to know he's very worried about your case."

* * *

"Nurse," asked the doctor, "why is your uniform undone and your hair all messed up?"

"I took that man's temperature like you told me to. Why didn't you say he was an anal erotic?"

* * *

Dr. Brackett stopped at the bedside of his wealthy male patient. "Nurse," he said to the pretty blonde nearby, "why isn't there a report made out? His chart is unmarked. How can I tell you whether my patient is showing improvement?"

"Oh, he is, Doctor. It's all in my diary," said the nurse.

* * *

McCarthy was recovering nicely from an operation, and he was happy except for his diet.

The meals were the same each day. For breakfast there was always a glass of apple juice, one egg, one piece of toast and the ever-present urinal bottle.

One morning, to relieve his boredom, McCarthy ate the toast and the egg but poured the juice into the urinal bottle.

Miss Prescott, the ''we'' nurse, arrived and asked, ''Did *we* enjoy breakfast?'' Then looking at the bottle, she said, ''*We* must have been a bad boy because this looks a little cloudy.''

''Well, then *we* better run it through again!'' said McCarthy, raising the bottle to his lips.

* * *

Hospital Hijinks

A patient gazed fondly at the really stacked girl in white beside the bed. "Wonderful nurse you've got here," he told the doctor. "One touch of her hands cooled my fever immediately."

"I know," said the doctor, "I could hear her slap you way down the end of the hall."

* * *

Adele, a very attractive and saucy nurse, joined the staff on the ninth floor, and soon the nurses began gossiping about her.

"Why don't you girls like her?" asked the receptionist. "She seems so efficient."

"Sure," snarled the supervisor, "she's so efficient she can make a patient without disturbing the bed!"

101

Miss McConnell, the head nurse of the hospital maternity ward, was making her rounds and stopped to look in on the nursery. Most of the newborn infants looked the same but she noticed one that seemed particularly puny and shriveled.

"He's one of the artificially inseminated babies brought in yesterday," explained the attending nurse.

"Confirms a pet theory of mine," said Miss McConnell, "Spare the rod and spoil the child!"

* * *

"I was in the hospital for just a minor operation," complained Charlene, "but they drove me nuts."

"I know what you mean," said her friend. "After a while, I got suspicious of everybody. Every time I heard a knock on the door I'd ask, 'Who goes there—friend or enema?' "

* * *

Two student nurses were slipping out through the side door of the hospital just as two interns were sneaking in. The corridor clock chimed 3:00 A.M.

"Sh-h," whispered the interns, "we've been out after hours."

"Sh-h, yourself," said the nurses, "we're going out after ours."

Doctor: Ask the accident victim his name so we can notify his family.

Nurse: (after consultation with patient): He says his family knows his name.

* * *

Bannon had a private room at St. Francis. As he lay in his bed battered and bandaged, his friend Campbell came to visit and wanted to know what was wrong.

"I got seenus trouble."

"You mean sinus trouble, don't you?"

"No," moaned Bannon, "I was making love to a guy's wife and he seen us!"

* * *

Kirk had some minor surgery done, and the day after the operation his buddy Lou stopped by for a visit. As Lou watched, a steady stream of nurses came in to fluff his pillow, offer to give him a back rub and ask if there was anything else he needed. "Why all the attention?" asked Lou. "Let's face it—you're not in serious condition."

"I know," smiled Kirk, "but the girls sort of formed a fan club when word got out that I needed 32 stitches for my circumcision?"

* * *

Phil Sterling, the talented TV actor, tells this titillating tall tale:

Andrews had been in a bad auto accident, and his arms and legs were in casts and his ribs taped. He was so bandaged up that he could hardly move. Dr. Anstead instructed the nurse to take the patient's temperature every 15 minutes and chart it.

The nurse gave Andrews a rectal thermometer and left the room for a few minutes. When she returned she was astounded to discover the thermometer in the patient's mouth.

"How did you ever get it there?" she asked, "it's impossible for you to move!"

Andrews winked and said, "I hiccupped!"

* * *

Goodwin, age 62, was rushed to the hospital and given pain killers and sedatives. But they didn't help, and his screams disturbed the other patients.

Then, suddenly, instead of shrieks of pain, a nurse heard loud sounds coming from his room. She found Goodwin jumping up and down on his bed singing at the top of his lungs. She ran out and said to a doctor, "That patient doesn't belong in the medical ward. He should be in psychiatry. He's in there singing, 'A tisket, a tasket, a green and yellow basket.' "

The doctor visited Goodwin and then reported to the nurse, "He's all right. He was supposed to be operated on for a stone in his kidney and he was just singing, 'I pissed it, I passed it. Am I a lucky bastard!' "

* * *

"How was the hospital?"

"Great! The guy next to me had a fever of 104 degrees, so they put him in a bed with a girl who had the chills."

* * *

*   *   *

Pelton, who had been confined to his bed a long time, decided to have some fun with Miss Dobbs, the straitlaced circulating nurse. Pelton said to her, "Where does a woman's hair grow thickest and blackest and curliest?"

Miss Dobbs turned beet-red and ran from the room. She returned immediately with the head nurse, an old sourpuss.

"Young man, before I have you thrown out, tell me what you said, because Nurse Dobbs is too upset to repeat it."

"Certainly, I simply asked her where does a girl's hair grow thickest and blackest and curliest."

"And where *does* it?" asked the old battle-axe.

"Why, in Central Africa, of course!"

*   *   *

Hanson was recovering nicely. Each day from his bed he pinched the day nurse's behind and made lewd remarks.

"With your mind," she said, "you should be living in a whore house."

"At these prices, I could afford to!" exclaimed Hanson.

Elliot Kaplan, the jovial New Jersey internist, relates this rollicking roaster:

One evening Eula Mae strolled into the Jersey City Medical Center Emergency Room and asked to see the "*up*turn."

"I think," said the nurse, "you mean the *in*tern, right?"

"Guess so," said Eula Mae. "I wanna get a contamination."

"You mean *ex*amination," corrected the nurse.

"Okay. But I wanna go to the fraternity ward."

"I'm sure," said the nurse, "that you're thinking of the *ma*ternity ward."

"Uptern, intern . . . contamination, examination . . . fraternity, maternity, what difference does it make!" said the girl. "I only know that I ain't demonstrated in two months and I think I'm stagnant!"

* * *

O'Shaughnessy was in the hospital for a complete checkup. At 11 A.M., they brought him a bowl of soup, which he refused. At noon they brought another bowl, which he also turned down. At 2:00 they tried again and once more he said no to the soup. At 6:00 P.M. they served him soup for dinner, and he sent it back. They tried again at 10:00. Once more he refused the soup. Then

108

during the night he was awakened and given an enema.

The next day, his wife came to visit him. "How they been treatin' you, darlin'?" she asked.

"Okay," he answered. "But Maggie, if you ever have to stay in a hospital and they offer you soup, take it. Otherwise at night while you're asleep, they come in and shove it up your ass!"

* * *

Dr. Endoso stood at his patient's bedside and tried to soothe him. "Don't worry, Mr. Robles! Within six weeks of amputating your legs I will have you on your feet again!"

* * *

Shelby was healing quickly after his serious operation, and this was the first day on a special diet. The nurse fed him one teaspoonful of instant pudding, a thimbleful of tea, and a protein cracker measuring a quarter-inch square. "Is that all I get?" he protested.

"That's all," answered the nurse. "Is there anything else I can do for you?"

"Yeah," said Shelby. "Bring me a postage stamp. I'd like to read."

* * *

Barry Unger, the dynamic Beverly Hills internist, delights patients with this dazzler:

Cynthia, a voluptuous brassiere model, was about to undergo a minor operation. She had been wheeled along to the operating room door, where the nurse left her to find out if the staff was ready.

Suddenly, a young man in a white coat came up to the trolley, lifted the sheet, examined her closely and walked away, nodding his head. Another man did the same thing and also left without comment.

When a third appeared and pulled back the sheet, Cynthia exclaimed, "What's the point of all this last-minute observation. Aren't you ready to operate?"

"No idea, lady," replied the young man. "We're just painting the corridor."

Rhodes, a young navy doctor, was stationed aboard an aircraft carrier cruising the Indian Ocean. One day he diagnosed the illness of a seaman but wasn't sure he had the facilities to treat it. Rhodes wired the nearest base hospital:

HAVE A CASE OF BERIBERI.
WHAT SHALL I DO?

A prankster at the hospital radioed back,

GIVE IT TO THE MARINES.
THEY'LL DRINK ANYTHING.

* * *

Larry Carr, the Bakersfield Memorial Hospital prexy, cracks up golf buddies with this beaut:

A mid-west hospital's Purchasing Department head was checking on some supplies that had recently arrived. He phoned the laboratory and spoke to a member of the research staff.

"That new microscope I ordered for you—is it powerful enough?"

"Is it?" exclaimed the technician, "I just saw two germs screwing!"

* * *

* * *

Werner, who was subject to blackouts and convulsions, collapsed on the street one afternoon. An emergency ambulance rushed him to the nearest hospital, where a physician made a cursory examination and ordered an immediate operation. As the operating room was being prepared a nurse, going through Werner's clothing, found this note pinned to his wallet:

This is to let the house surgeon know that I am undergoing a plain case of convulsions. It is not appendicitis. My appendix has already been removed three times.

* * *

Jameson, the hospital supervisor, sent for a young surgeon and complimented him on his efforts in the operating room that morning. "Marvelous bit of work," said the institution head. "You operated just in time. One more day and the patient would have recovered without it."

* * *

113

Abe Rein, New York's foremost furrier, found this tickling tidbit:

Finley lay quietly as five doctors held a conference around his bedside. When they left, he became so upset that the nurse sent for the senior resident, Dr. Lacy.

"Now what's all this about?" asked Lacy. "Why have you got yourself all worked up?"

"It was that conference," panted Finley. "There must be an awful lot of doubt about what's wrong with me."

"Not at all," asserted the doctor. "Where did you get that idea?"

"You had that big argument about the diagnosis. All the other doctors disagreed with you, didn't they?"

"To some extent," said Lacy. "But I'll bet you the post-mortem proves I was right."

*   *   *

 r. Middleton, the new

intern on duty at the hospital emergency room, answered the phone late one night. "Doctor," exclaimed a woman, "what shall I do? We just discovered our two-year-old son has eaten a whole tube of contraceptive jelly."

"Well," replied the intern, "if it's really an emergency, why don't you have one of the all-night drugstores deliver another tube?"

* * *

Lochridge stormed into the pharmacy and began shouting at the druggist.

"You made a mistake in that prescription you gave me for my wife. Instead of quinine you used strychnine!"

"In that case," said the pharmacist, "you owe me $10 more."

Druggist: Well, Jonathan, did that mud-pack improve your wife's appearance?

Jonathan: It did for a few days—but then it wore off.

* * *

Mrs. Steckman was giving a formal dinner party and sent an invitation to Dr. Morrison, the city's leading internist.

In reply, she received an absolutely illegible note. "I don't know if he accepted or refused," she told a friend. "I can't read this note."

"Take it to a pharmacy," said her friend. "No matter how badly written, a druggist can always read a doctor's handwriting."

The pharmacist looked at the piece of paper, disappeared into the back room and returned in a few minutes with a small bottle. "Here you are," he said, "that'll be $16.80!"

* * *

"I understand Rifkin has been given a medal by the Society for Pharmaceutical Research."

"That's right. He invented three new sandwiches."

116

*   *   *

At a Chicago medical convention two pharmaceutical salesmen were discussing a mutual acquaintance.

"Max is a great druggist, isn't he?"

"Yeah, but I think he puts too much salt in the egg salad."

*   *   *

Roderick ran into a Rexall Pharmacy and shouted to the man behind the drug counter, "I'm poisoned! It must've been the sandwiches my wife gave me."

"Of course," replied the druggist. "You're taking a chance every time you eat a sandwich that isn't prepared by a registered pharmacist."

*   *   *

Delahanty: A mustard plaster, please.
Drug clerk: We're out of mustard. How about mayonnaise?

*   *   *

"Has putting in that lunch counter helped your business?" asked Townsend.

"Well," answered the druggist, "it's tripled the sales on Alka-Seltzer."

117

Quentin, a regular customer of the small town drugstore, struck up a conversation with the owner. "Anything new from the scientific boys?"

"Yeah," answered the druggist. "We got a new wonder drug that's so powerful, you gotta be in perfect health to take it."

* * *

It won't be long now! Very soon, we can expect to see the restaurants retaliate by putting in a line of drugs and toilet articles.

* * *

Jack Ginsberg, the dashing Chicago druggist, delivers this delightful dandy:

Myron, son of the local baker, rushed into the bakery one morning and said, "Dad, there's a bill collector at the house, and Mom says come right over and pay him."

"Which merchant is trying to collect?"

"I don't know, Dad."

"Well, son, run home and whisper in Mama's ear that if it's Tobias, the tailor, hide my cigars because he'll grab a handful; if it's Bleeker, the butcher, tell her to hide my bottle of whiskey on the pantry shelf because he'll finish the bottle. If it's Decker, the druggist, you better sit on your mother's lap until I get there."

* * *

Kertley walked into Dubin's Drugstore and said to the owner, "Make me a malted!"

"Okay," said Dubin, "Poof, you're a malted!"

* * *

Susan Glazer, California's glamorous pharmacist, gets gaffaws with this goony giggler:

Grubbs puffed heavily on his cigar while loitering in the shopping mall drugstore.

The pharmacist had to speak forcefully to him. "Please, sir, there's no smoking."

"But I just bought the cigar here."

"Look" pleaded the druggist, "we also sell laxatives here, but you can't enjoy them on the premises."

* * *

Bernstein rushed into a Brooklyn pharmacy and said to the clerk behind the counter, "Do you do urinanalysis here?"

"Yea," said the clerk.

"Then wash your hands good and make me a chocolate egg cream."

* * *

119

IF DRUGS AND PHYSIC COULD BUT SAVE
US MORTALS FROM THE DREARY GRAVE,
'TIS KNOWN THAT I TOOK FULL ENOUGH
OF THE APOTHECARIES' STUFF
TO HAVE PROLONGED LIFE'S BUSY FEAST
TO A FULL CENTURY AT LEAST;
BUT SPITE OF ALL THE DOCTORS' SKILL,
OF DAILY DRAUGHT AND NIGHTLY PILL,
READER, AS SURE AS YOU'RE ALIVE,
I WAS SENT HERE AT TWENTY-FIVE.

120

Customer: I can't sleep at night—the least little sound disturbs me. I'm a victim of insomnia. Even a cat on our back fence distresses me beyond words.

Druggist: This powder will be effective.

Customer: When do I take it?

Druggist: You don't. Give it to the cat in milk.

* * *

Lewis Marks, the dashing New Jersey druggist, loves this delightful dab of drollery:

Hanahan sat down at the soda fountain in the corner drugstore. "What flavors do you have in ice cream?"

The teenage girl's throat was inflamed, and she answered in a hoarse whisper, "Vanilla, strawberry, and butter pecan."

"You got laryngitis?"

"No," she whispered, "just vanilla, strawberry, and butter pecan."

* * *

Heath, a shy little man, stepped up to the druggist. "Is it possible to fix castor oil so it can't be tasted?"

"Sure," said the pharmacist, "and while you're waiting, have a glass of root beer on me over at the soda fountain."

Heath crossed to the counter and gratefully accepted the drink. "How did it taste?" asked the pharmacist.

"That's the best glass of root beer I've ever had."

"Well, the castor oil was in it. Which proves it's possible to fix it without tasting it."

"But it was my wife who wanted the castor oil," said the little man.

* * *

In Kansas City a pharmacist filled a prescription for an old friend.

"Let me know if this stuff does any good, Neville. I've got rheumatism myself."

* * *

Scene: Pharmacy. Foster is looking at shelves.

A woman approaches him.

Woman: Can I help you, sir?

Foster: I'd like to see the registered pharmacist.

Woman: I'm a registered pharmacist, and so is my sister. We own the store.

Foster: Well . . . I guess you can help me. I've had this tremendous erection for two weeks and nothing I do will get rid of it. What can you give me for it?

Woman: That's a rather unusual problem. I'll have to consult with my sister.

She goes into the back room and returns in a few minutes.

Woman: How about $5000 and half the business.

* * *

Dennis Kane, the pharmacist turned movie producer, found this little fun filler:

A newspaper reporter was doing a story about how people depend on the neighborhood drugstore. He interviewed the owner. "Do people mix themselves up when they come in here?"

"I'll say they do!" said the old pharmacist. "They ask me for paralyzed gauze; aspiration tablets; polluted water; Scott's emotion; cynical thermometers. But the payoff was the woman who came in the other day and said she wanted a box of exorbitant cotton. You know, looking at today's prices, maybe she was right."

123

Mrs. Tolbert became incensed when the druggist informed her that her favorite cure-all could not be bought without a prescription.

"Lady," explained the druggist, "you can't have this except by prescription because it is habit-forming."

"It is not," screamed the distraught woman. "I ought to know. I've been taking it regularly for seventeen years."

* * *

Benson had been drinking at the corner saloon. On his way home he staggered into a drugstore and said to Dickey, the druggist, "My wife asked me to get something for her, and I forgot what it is!"

"Well, you just go home and sleep it off," said Dickey, "and then you'll remember what it is!"

"No," said Benson, "if my wife doesn't get what she wants, she'll kill me. Maybe you can help me remember!"

"What do you want me to do?"

"Name some states!"

"OK, there's . . . New York, New Jersey, New Hampshire, Vermont."

"Not yet. It doesn't strike a familiar note."

"Then there's North Carolina, South Carolina, Georgia, Virginia . . ."

"No, keep going!"

". . . Indiana, Illinois, Ohio, Minnesota, Michigan. . . ."

"You're warm! Name some of the cities in Michigan!"

"Well, there's Saginaw, Flint, Pontiac, Lansing, Battle Creek, Detroit!"

"Wait a minute, Detroit's on a lake. Name the five great lakes!"

"There's Lake Huron, Lake Michigan, Lake Superior, Lake Ontario, Lake Erie!"

"We're gettin' close. What happened in 1813 on Lake Erie?"

"Well, the British fleet was destroyed there by Admiral Perry!"

"That's it!" exclaimed the drunk. "I want 60 cents' worth of Perrigoric!"

* * *

A pretty University of Connecticut co-ed dropped into a Hartford drugstore and said to the druggist, "I want to buy a vibrator!"

"Okay," said the pharmacist, "come this way."

"If I could come that way I wouldn't need the vibrator!" quipped the campus cutie.

* * *

Mrs. Silverstein's son had to attend a special pharmacists' meeting one evening, so she agreed to work in his Brooklyn drugstore. Old man Zucker wandered into the store and said, "How much you charge for a box Alka-Selzter?"

"$1.50," said Mrs. Silverstein.

"What?" exclaimed Zucker. "Every other drugstore in Brooklyn I could get for ninety cents."

"All the other stores are closed now. You want it or don't you?"

"How much is a bottle bicarbonate of soda?"

"$4.85," said the druggist's mother.

"Are you nuts?" shouted Zucker. "Any place you go in this city you could get it for $2.25."

"Listen, we're the only store open. Take it or leave it."

The old man bought the bicarbonate, and as Mrs. Silverstein leaned over the counter Zucker could clearly see the woman's breasts.

"What's that?" he asked.

"What do you mean, what's that?" said the woman. "That's my bosoms. What did you think it was?"

"Well," said the senior citizen, "everything else here is so high, I thought it was your ass!"

* * *

Quack Quickies

Shankland was a grouchy, ill-tempered old practitioner. He sat behind his desk and glared at the new patient.

"Have you been to a doctor before you came to me?" he asked.

"No, sir," said the man. "I went to a pharmacist."

"That shows how much sense some people have," growled Shankland. "What kind of dumb advice did he give you?"

"He told me to come to see you."

"Gee, Doc, I don't know what to do. Whenever I lift my arm it pains me terribly."

"Then don't lift it."

*   *   *

Did you hear about the sensitive young doctor who refused to visit the farmer again until he gagged his ducks?

*   *   *

Mrs. Bentley telephoned a doctor frantically. "Please! My husband's at death's door."

"Now don't get excited," said the M.D. "I'll be right over and pull him through."

*   *   *

"What is it, Nurse?"

"Doctor, this is the third operating table you've ruined this month. Please don't cut so deep."

*   *   *

Koster had an operation and was coming out of the ether. He looked at the two other patients in nearby beds and said, "Thank God that's over!"

‘ "Don't be too sure," said Benson in the next bed, "they left a sponge in me and had to cut me open again."

Rankin in a bed on the other side of Koster added, "They had to open me up too, to recover one of their instruments."

Just then the doctor stuck his head in the door and called, "Anyone seen my hat?"

Koster fainted.

* * *

A very sucessful Beverly Hills plastic surgeon bought a palatial home and appropriately named it BEDSIDE MANOR.

* * *

Did you hear about the doctor who felt the patient's purse and decided there was no hope?

* * *

Salisbury began shouting at his physician, "You're nothing but a quack. You've had me come back for unnecessary treatments for six months. You've taken my money without helping me. You've gotten rich on my case alone!"

"That's gratitude," said the M.D. "And to think I named my new yacht after you."

Abe Harris, Rocky River's resident druggist, entertains customers with this apocryphal anecdote on pharmaceutical history:

Dr. Mobelsby, the quack medicine man, pulled into a small town and quickly had a crowd gathered around him. "Folks, this little bottle of magic is the elixir of life," he said. "For only one dollar it will help you live to be great-great-great-grandparents. Just look at me. I am the picture of health, and friends, I am over 230 years old!"

While Mobelsby talked, Peckham, his assistant, circulated through the crowd, collecting the dollar bills for the bottles of colored sugar water. One of the onlookers stopped him. "Is that man really over 230 years old?" he asked.

"You can't prove it by me," said Peckham as he took the rube's buck. "I've only worked for him 110 years myself."

"I was in such great pain, Doctor, that I wanted to die."

"You did right, Mrs. Tyler, to call for me."

*   *   *

Late one afternoon Dr. Whitlock motioned the last couple in the waiting room into his office. It had been a tough day, and the physician wanted to get this last patient over with quickly. She complained of abdominal pain, but the M.D. couldn't get her to answer directly. She would not speak above a whisper. Finally, Whitlock got her onto the examining table and into the stirrups.

The minute the examination was over the woman leaped off the table, got into her clothes and quickly ran from the room.

"Anybody that can get out of here that fast can't be very sick," said the doctor to the man. "I'm sure your wife will be all right."

"She's not my wife," said the man. "I was wondering why you called me in with her."

*   *   *

Did you hear about the doctor who became a bank robber but failed because nobody could read his handwriting on the holdup note?

132

* * *

Emile Ravdin, the lovable Los Angeles ophthalmologist, poses this rib-tickling risibility:

Did you hear about the eyeglasses maker who moved his shop to an island off Alaska and is now known as an optical Aleutian?

* * *

Annette, a pretty bookkeeper, went to Dr. Lacy, an optometrist, to test her vision. "I don't use a chart," he announced. "Would you stand up at the wall?"

After she walked to the other side of the room, the optometrist held his hands above his head and asked, "What am I doing?"

Annette squinted and answered, "I can't tell."

Then Lacy folded his arms on his chest and asked her again what he was doing.

"I really can't see," she admitted.

Then the optometrist opened his trousers, pulled out his penis and asked, "What's this?"

"That's your organ!" Annette replied.

"That's it, Miss," said the quack. "You're cockeyed!"

* * *

SIGN IN AN OPTOMETRIST'S WINDOW

If you don't see what you want, you've come to the right place.

* * *

"I've been seeing spots in front of my eyes."

"Have you seen a doctor?"

"No, just spots."

* * *

Jay Fleischmann, the famous St. Louis ophthalmologist, finds this fable a bunch of fun:

Mrs. Grabowski came into the room. "Doctor," she said. "Tell me what's wrong with me."

"I can tell you three things," he said. "First, you're too fat. Second, your teeth could stand some dental work. And third, you need glasses. If you took a good look at the sign outside, you would have seen that I'm a doctor of divinity."

* * *

Did you hear about the man who swallowed his glass eye and rushed to a stomach specialist?

The doctor stared down the fellow's throat and said, "I've looked into a lot of stomachs in my time, but this is the first one that ever looked back at me."

* * *

"How did the operation go?" asked the anxious wife.

"It was a complete success," said the surgeon, "until your husband fell off the table."

* * *

Dr. Farnum leaned over the man, tapped his chest, and listened.

"Say," asked the patient, "why do you do that?"

"I don't know," said the M.D. "I saw it in the movies."

* * *

Langston went to a new doctor. "Come over here," said the M.D. "Hang your head out of the window and stick your tongue out."

Langston did as he was told, then pulled his head back in and said, "What was that test for?"

"It wasn't a test," said the quack.

"Then what did you make me do that for?"

"I hate my neighbors."

Steven Lake, the prominent California plastic surgeon, gets chuckles with this perfect pleasantry:

Dr. Stoner loved a downtown Chicago steak house. One day he parked his car in front of a fire hydrant outside the restaurant and put a note on the windshield reading:

Doctor working inside.

When he finished his lunch and returned to the car, Stoner found a parking ticket on the windshield with a note attached reading:

Policeman working outside.

Did you hear about the gynecologist who left his profession because he could never see eye to eye with his patients?

* * *

BONE SPECIALIST

Arthur Itis

* * *

Constance and a man she just met at a party were in bed in a motel. They were locked in a passionate embrace when she suddenly exclaimed, "What I'm doing is strictly against doctor's orders."

"What's wrong, baby? Are you ill?"

"No, I'm married to a doctor."

* * *

Thatcher had been in a terrible auto accident.

After two days in a coma, he woke up and found the surgeon standing beside his hospital bed.

"I have bad and good news for you," said the surgeon. "The bad news is that I cut off your good leg by mistake."

"Oh, Jesus!" exclaimed Thatcher. "Now tell me the good part."

"The good news is that your bad leg is getting well."

Dr. Russell rushed into the bedroom and said to his wife, "Quick, get me my bag!"

"What's the matter?" she asked.

"Some fellow just phoned and said he couldn't live without me."

"Wait a moment," said the wife. "I think that call was for me."

* * *

Dr. Yates had just performed a difficult operation. As the nurse watched in awe, the surgeon unscrewed the wooden hand he had been using.

"Marvelous!" she murmured.

"That's nothing!" said the doctor, unscrewing a wooden leg.

"But how did you ever manage to overcome such handicaps?"

"Come on down to my office and I'll show you!"

She went down to his office and he screwed his head off.

* * *

Jessup came home unexpectedly and found the doctor in bed with his wife. "What do you think you're doing?" asked the husband.

"I'm, er, taking your wife's temperature!" stammered the M.D.

"Okay," said Jessup, "but that thing better have numbers on it when you take it out!"

* * *

Eunice went to a gynecologist for artificial insemination. After she assumed the proper position atop the examining table, the M.D. unzipped himself.

"Doctor," exclaimed the woman, "what are you doing?"

"I'm sorry, Miss," replied the doctor, "but I'm all out of the bottled stuff. You'll have to settle for draft."

* * *

Dr. Whitcomb was examining a pretty New York high fashion model.

"My, you have a big vagina! My, you have a big vagina!"

"Oh, Doctor," retorted the girl, "you didn't have to repeat it!"

"I didn't!" said the M.D.

* * *

Urologists don't have to advertise. They just open up an office and the patients come trickling in.

* * *

Mrs. Hatcher had a colonic obstruction and was being massaged rectally by a physician. Suddenly she said, "Doctor, are you sure that's your finger?"

"If it isn't," replied the internist, "I'm sure as hell in the wrong hole!"

* * *

A Hollywood specialist met a country doctor while on vacation in Canada.

"In your city, Doctor," asked the rural physician, "what is the most widely used means of avoiding having babies?"

"As far as I knew," said the movie-land medico, "the girls just spit them out."

* * *

Wife:	I went to the doctor today and he said I might be pregnant!
Husband:	That's ridiculous! I've had a vasectomy.
Wife:	Yes, but he hasn't.

* * *

Bill Leyton, the retired Sea Ranch pediatrician, loves this lulu:

Mrs. Crawford was seriously ill. Her husband sent for Dr. Hill, the only M.D. within 30 miles. The M.D. dashed inside the sickroom and came out a minute later asking for a chisel. Crawford was stunned but so anxious he didn't ask questions. He found a chisel.

Ten minutes later, the doctor poked his head out and asked, "You got a hammer?"

The husband was puzzled, but he rushed down to the cellar and frantically brought him a hammer. Five minutes later Dr. Hill came out stripped to the waist, sweat pouring from his body and said, "You got a hacksaw?"

By now, Crawford was beside himself. "For God's sake," he screamed . . . "You wanted a hammer, then a chisel, now a hacksaw. What are you doing to my wife."

"Nothing yet," said the M.D. "Can't get my instrument bag open."

* * *

Did you hear about the doctor who discovered a cure for which there was no disease?

* * *

Madeline went to the doctor for her annual checkup. He told her to disrobe and climb onto the examination table.

"Doctor," she said shyly, "I'm sorry, but I can't undress right in front of you."

"All right," said the physician, "I'll flick off the lights. You undress and tell me when you're through."

The room was completely dark. "Doctor, I've undressed," said Madeline. "What should I do with my clothes?"

"Your clothes?" answered the quack. "Put them over here, on top of mine."

* * *

Here lieth an innocent maid
By a medical student betrayed
    Caesarean section
    Came after injection,
She thought he was teaching First Aid.

* * *

A con man put up a sign in Harlem:
YOU CAN BE ANYTHING—$20.

Dickson came up to him and said, "I've always wanted to be a Doctor."

"All right," said the flim-flammer. "Take this diploma. You're now a doctor."

Dickson opened an office. His first patient, Miss Jackson, weighed 350 pounds. Dickson put his stethoscope next to her stomach, listened for a moment, and then announced, "You have a locked bowel."

"Man, you're crazy," exclaimed Miss Jackson. "I've had the diarrhea for eight years."

"The diagnosis is still correct," announced the man. "You have a locked bowel, but it's in the locked *open* position."

* * *

Patient Persilflage

Herman the hypochondriac began sobbing before a doctor. "I'm sure I've got a liver disease, and I'm gonna die from it."

"Ridiculous," said the doctor. "You'd never know if you had the disease or not. With that ailment there's no discomfort of any kind."

"Right," said Herman, "those are my exact symptoms."

* * *

Dr. Stevens examined a new patient very carefully. After studying the X-rays, he said to the man, "Could you pay for an operation if I told you it was necessary?"

"Would you find one necessary if I told you I couldn't pay for it?"

Mrs. Green and Mrs. Becke sat beside each other at a Palm Springs hotel pool.

"You ought to try my doctor," said Mrs. Green. "He's marvelous!"

"Why should I see your doctor?" asked Mrs. Becke. "There's nothing wrong with me."

"Oh!" replied Mrs. Green. "My doctor's wonderful. He'll find something!"

* * *

Mrs. Slagel complained to a doctor about a stomach problem. "What did you eat for dinner last night?" asked the M.D.

"Oysters," she said.

"Fresh oysters?"

"How should I know?" said Mrs. Slagel.

"Well," asked the doctor, "couldn't you tell when you took off the shells?"

"Good heavens," she gasped. "Are you supposed to take off the shells?"

* * *

Michael Jackson, California's consummate radio talk-show host, broke up listeners with this lulu:

McGuire had a complete physical by the doctor and was told he had a flucky. McGuire trudged home in abject depression. "What's the matter?" asked his wife.

148

"The doctor said I had a flucky," he replied.

"What's a flucky?"

"I don't know."

"Don't you think you ought to find out what it is?" charged Mrs. McGuire.

- McGuire rushed back to the doctor and said, "Please, Doc, you gotta tell me. What's a flucky?"

"I don't know." answered the M.D.

"B-but . . ." stammered McGuire, "after my exam you told me I had a flucky."

"I certainly did not!" snapped the physician. "I said that you got off lucky."

* * *

Young Doctor Forbes completed an examination of an elderly man.

"Tell me," asked the M.D. "Do you suffer from arthritis?"

"Of course!" snarled the senior citizen. "What the hell else can I do with it?"

* * *

"How do you feel?" asked the doctor. "Sort of sluggish?"

"Sluggish?" answered the patient. "If I felt that good I wouldn't even be here!"

* * *

Comic Ewald Breuer says, "I decided to change my physician when I found out he'd been treating a patient for ten years for yellow jaundice before he found out the man was Chinese."

* * *

"I had an operation, and the doctor left a sponge in me."

"Got any pain?"

"No, but boy, do I ever get thirsty!"

* * *

The doctor was very pleased with his patient's progress. "You're coughing more easily this morning."

"Well, I ought to. I've been practicng all night."

* * *

Mrs. Farrington argued with her doctor that his bill was too high.

"Don't forget," said the medic, "that I visited Melvin nine times when he had the measles."

"And don't you forget," she replied, "that Melvin made you lots of money by giving the measles to the whole fifth grade!"

* * *

150

"What about my bill?" asked Dr. Harsen.

"I can't pay it," said Gridley, "but if you'll take me down your cellar, I'll show you how to fix your meter so you can gyp the gas company."

* * *

A singular fellow of Weston
Has fifty feet of intestine;
    Though a signal success
    In the medical press
It isn't much good for digestin'.

* * *

Gwen sat despondently in Dr. Baer's office. He handed her a prescription and said, "From now on, I want you to do everything I tell you."

"That's what my boyfriend told me," retorted Gwen, "and that's why I'm here."

* * *

Alice: I saw a doctor today about my nymphomania.
Fran: What did he do?
Alice: Made me pay in advances.

* * *

Pauline came home after a visit to the doctor and told her parents, "The rash between my legs is nothing to worry about—it's only whisker burns."

* * *

"How's your husband?"

"No different. He always feels bad when he feels good for fear he'll feel worse when he feels better."

* * *

Rembold told the doctor he wanted a vasectomy. "All right," said the medic, "but have you discussed the operation and its implications with your wife and family?"

"Yes," said the man. "I'm not really thrilled about it, but my wife asked the children to vote on it."

"What was the outcome?" asked the doctor.

"The kids favored it, eleven to three."

* * *

Karen: The doctor says I have nymphomania.

Irene: Who are you taking for it?

Pearl was shocked at the doctor's announcement. "I can't possibly be pregnant. I'm not married, have no boyfriends, I've never even been near a man except . . . oh, . . . that lifeguard told me it was a new form of artificial resuscitation."

* * *

A woman was in the doctor's office arranging for her fourth abortion.

"I hope you don't think I'm too personal," said the doctor, "but is this the same man who was responsible for your three other pregnancies?"

"The same."

"Well," continued the doctor, "how come you don't marry him?"

"To tell you the truth, Doctor, he doesn't appeal to me!"

* * *

Gonzales wanted to make his new wife pregnant. "How you do that?" he asked the doctor.

"Put the longest thing you've got in the hairiest thing your wife has," said the M.D.

Two months later the doctor asked, "How're you doing?"

"Well," he said. "I stick my nose in her armpit every night, but no luck yet."

Sanchez boarded a San Diego bus, his hands outstretched and held apart from his body. He said to the driver, "Take the 50 cents from this right pocket and place a transfer in the left pocket." His hands were still held out in that rigid position.

"What's the matter, you paralyzed?" asked the driver.

"No. The doctor ordered a bedpan for my wife, and I don't want to lose the measurement."

* * *

Doc: Does your penis burn after intercourse?

Patient: I don't know. I never tried
lighting it.

* * *

Tillie had recently married, and now she was complaining to the doctor. "You gotta help me. Ever since you outfitted me with this diaphragm I urinate purple."

"Hm-m-m, what kind of jelly do you use?" asked the M.D.

"Grape!" said the new bride.

* * *

Mrs. Ogden went to her doctor and said, "Please give me a prescription for the Pill."

"I don't think you need the Pill at your age."

"It relaxes me."

"But you know the *purpose* of the Pill. It's not for relaxing," exclaimed the physician.

"I know," said Mrs. Ogden, "but my daughter dates, and every morning I drop one in her orange juice. *Believe me,* I feel more relaxed."

Doctor: I don't like the looks of your husband.

Wife: I don't either, but he's good to the children.

* * *

Pierson phoned his doctor and shouted, "My six-year-old son just swallowed a contraceptive!"

"Keep calm. I'll come right over."

As the M.D. prepared to leave his office, the phone rang. It was Pierson again. "Forget it, Doc, I found another one!"

* * *

"Doctor, I don't know what's wrong with me. Every morning at 7 o'clock I have a bowel movement."

"What's wrong with that?"

"I don't get out of bed until 9 o'clock."

* * *

Laura and Ceil, two Detroit stenos, were having lunch, and Laura confided that she was going to have a baby.

"What makes you so sure?" asked Ceil.

"I should know," said Laura, "after all, I've been under my doctor for the past two months."

* * *

Constance climbed on the gynecologist's table. "Just relax, dear," he said, removing her panties. "There's nothing to worry about."

"Maybe not," she murmured, "but this'll be the first time I've ever had a doctor look *up* my throat."

* * *

Kenney had been given a prostatic massage by a medic. The following week his wife said, "Why pay the doctor? I can do it. Just tell me how."

"It's real easy," he said, "I just bend over with my pants down and he puts one hand on my shoulder, and then with the other hand . . . hold it. Now that I think about it, that son-of-a-bitch had both hands on my shoulders!"

* * *

"I believe time heals everything."

"Yeah? You never tried sitting it out in my doctor's waiting room?"

* * *

There was a smart miss with a hernia
Who said to her doctor, "Goldernia,
    When improving my middle
    Be sure you don't fiddle
With matters that do not concernia."

* * *

Patti, a well-stacked blonde, sat on the examining table. Dr. Donovan placed his hand on her bare breast. "You know what I'm doing, don't you?" he asked.

"Yes," she murmured, "You're checking for breast cancer."

Donovan then began caressing her stomach. "Of course," he continued, "you know what I'm doing."

"Yes," she smiled. "You're checking my appendix."

By now the M.D. couldn't control himself any longer. He ripped off his clothes and began making love to her. "You know what I'm doing, don't you?" he gasped.

"Yes," she replied. "You're checking for VD . . . and that's what I came here for."

* * *

* * *

Dr. Bristow finished examining Mrs. Lopez and said to her husband, "Your wife just needs more intercourse!"

"Intercourse—what's that?" he asked.

"Here, I'll show you," said the doctor. He then proceeded to make love to the woman right in front of the husband on the examination table.

"That's intercourse, heh?" said Lopez. "If I didn't know you were a doctor, I'd think you were screwing my wife!"

* * *

The coal miners were being examined by the company doctor. He was surprised to find a wad of chewing gum under each miner's foreskin.

"It is so dirty down in the mine, with coal dust," explained Kovak, "that this is the only clean place to put chewing gum."

The next man the medic examined had two wads of gum inside his foreskin.

"I'm keeping the other one for my friend who is still down in the mine," he explained.

* * *

* * *

Old Doc Masters passed away. A group of his friends decided to collect some money to give him a nice funeral. Their collection was not going well until they called on an eccentric old gentleman.

"How much were you hoping for from me?" he demanded.

"Fifty dollars, to bury the doctor," suggested their leader.

The old gentleman brought out his wallet and said, "Here's $300. Bury six of 'em."

* * *

The well-known surgeon wanted to establish some rapport with a man to whom he had given an estimate on a brain operation. "Your kids are no wilder than any of us when we were the same age," said the surgeon. "Why, when I was a boy I had a great ambition to be a pirate."

"You're lucky," said the patient, "not every man gets to be what he wants!"

* * *

161

A young woman with a baby was shown into the hospital clinic examination room. Doctor Oakes examined the baby, and then asked the woman, "Is he breast-fed or bottle-fed?"

"Breast-fed," she answered.

"Strip down to your waist," he ordered. She did and he examined her. He fingered her breasts. Then he squeezed and pulled them. Then he sucked on each nipple. Suddenly, he remarked, "No wonder this child is suffering from malnutrition. You don't have any milk."

"That's right," she replied. "It's my sister's child."

"I had no idea," said the M.D. "You shouldn't have come."

"I didn't till you started sucking on the second one."

Stanton was losing his hearing. Doctor Skantz told him it was caused by overindulgence sexually and that he must cut out women altogether or he would be stone deaf in two months.

Two months later Stanton had not come back, so the doctor phoned him.

"How are you doing?" asked the M.D.

"Eh? Who's this? Speak up, dammit!"

"It's Dr. Skantz," shouted the physician, "just called up to find out if your hearing had improved."

"No," shouted Stanton, "I'm deaf as a post. But nothing I was hearing made me feel half as good as getting laid."

* * *

Doctor: Say, the check you gave me for my bill came back.
Patient: So did my arthritis!

* * *

Balster was sitting in a doctor's waiting room, murmuring, "I hope I'm sick. I hope I'm sick."

"Hey," said the man across from him, "why do you hope you're sick?"

"I'd hate to be well and feel like this!"

* * *

Doctor:	Shall I give your wife a local anesthetic?
Wealthy Texan:	No. I'm rich. Give her the best. Give her something imported!

* * *

Carlton lay completely bandaged in his hospital room. He had to be fed rectally through a tube. One morning as a special treat, the nurse gave him coffee. Carlton began screaming through his bandages and tried to shove the tube away.

"What'sa matter?" asked the nurse. "Too hot?"

"No-no-no! Too much sugar!"

* * *

Old Mrs. Spinelli went to her physician and complained of constipation.

"Do you do anything about it?" asked the M.D.

"Of course I do. I sit on the toilet for three hours every day."

"No, no, I don't mean that. I mean do you take anything?"

"Of course," said the elderly woman, "I take along my knitting."

* * *

Barlow sat in the doctor's office. "My wife and I have been married ten years," he explained, "and lately our sex life isn't too good."

"Okay," said the medic, "here are some pills. Tonight before you go to sleep drop one in her coffee."

Later that evening Barlow followed the physician's orders. When his wife wasn't looking, he dropped a pill into her coffee. Then for good measure he decided to put one in his own drink.

An hour later they were fast asleep when suddenly Mrs. Barlow sat up in bed and moaned, "I want a man! I want a man!"

Barlow jumped up and shouted, "Me too! Me too!"

* * *

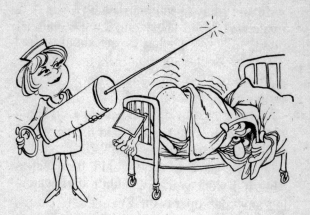

Medical Merriment

Dr. Bastion had just completed his 2000th successful operation. When he washed up, another doctor asked, "How did you accomplish such a remarkable feat!"

"It took a lot of patients!" replied the surgeon.

* * *

Baxter phoned a doctor frantically and screamed, "I swallowed a live bullet! What shall I do?"

"Eat a lot of baked beans," snapped the M.D., "and stand in front of your mother-in-law."

167

Nervous Patient:	Is this operation very dangerous, Doctor?
Surgeon:	That, my good man, is what we are about to find out.

*   *   *

"Tell me the truth," said the very sick man. "How long have I got?"

"It's hard to say," said the doctor, "but if I were you, I wouldn't start watching any soap operas on TV."

*   *   *

Al Zdenek, the witty Woodland Hills G.P., came up with this whimsical winner:

Dr. Elsdon stopped before the hospital bed of a lovely redhead.

"I'll have to give you a thorough examination," said the medic. "Will you please disrobe?"

"But Dr. Haber just examined me. And he found me perfect."

"Yes, he told me."

*   *   *

Dr. Beal was examining young Pierce. "Did I ever take out your tonsils?" he asked.

"No," said Pierce.

"Did I ever take out your appendix?" he asked.

"No," said the young man.

"Say, have you got a girlfriend named Maxine?"

"Yeah."

"I knew I took out something of yours!"

* * *

A doctor and his wife were walking on Fifth Avenue. A buxom brunette in tight-fitting sweater and skirt nodded hello from a nearby doorway.

"And who was that?" asked the wife.

"Oh, just a young woman I know professionally," said the doctor.

"I'm sure," said the wife, "but your profession or hers?"

* * *

Doctor: You're going to have to have an operation.

Patient: How much will it cost?

Doctor: $10,000.

Patient: Gosh, I don't have that kind of money.

Doctor: Tell you what I'll do. Give me $5,000 down and pay me $200 a month until the bill is paid.

Patient: That's just like buying a new car.

Doctor: I am.

Milt Hillman, the hearty Hollywood eye surgeon, loves this humorous dab of high-jinks:

Twelve-year-old Tommy enjoyed being the son of a surgeon. One day he and a friend were playing in the house where they discovered a skeleton in the closet of the examination room.

"What's that?" asked his friend.

"Oh, that," said Tommy, "that's Dad's first patient."

"Doctor, my feet hurt. When I leave here, what should I do?"

"Take a taxi," said the podiatrist.

* * *

Gardener woke up his doctor late one night and said, "I can't sleep. Can you do anything for me?"

"Hold the phone for awhile, and I'll sing you a lullaby," quipped the M.D.

* * *

"Tell me the truth, doctor," asked Perrott, "am I going to get well?"

"Of course you are," replied the doctor. "You're going to get well if it costs every cent you have."

* * *

Gallagher just had a heart transplant and was getting instructions from his doctor. He was placed on a strict diet, denied tobacco and alcohol, and advised to get at least eight hours' sleep a night.

"What about my sex life?" asked the patient. "Will it be all right for me to have intercourse?"

"Only with your wife," said the doctor. "We don't want you to get too excited."

"I want eight hundred dollars for the operation," said the doc.

"Can't you do it for four hundred?"

"Sure. But I'll use dull knives."

* * *

Larry Brown, the notable Newport Beach ENT specialist, supplied this nifty nugget of nonsense:

In reviewing his accounts Dr. Jenner realized the year had been a financial disaster. "I don't know why," he said to his wife, "but I had a lot more patients last year."

"I wonder where they could have gone?" she asked.

"We can only hope for the best," he replied.

* * *

Holden worked in a watch factory. One morning he had an unusual accident. He spilled some luminous paint on his crotch which seeped through his pants and covered his manhood. Next day Holden went to the company doctor and explained that his member glowed in the dark.

"What should I do, Doc?" he asked frantically.

"That's easy," replied the M.D. "Find yourself a woman who likes to sleep with a night light!"

Patient: Yes, I feel much better, thank you, doctor. But I'm still having trouble with my breathing.

Doctor: I'll just have to give you something to stop that.

* * *

Mrs. Kowalski complained that she was passing a lot of gas. "But," she said, "the fart does not make a noise." At that moment she presented the doctor with a sample.

He wrote out a prescription for suppositories.

"Will they clear up the blockage?" she asked.

"No, these will plug you up completely and make you fart louder. That way at least you'll hear them."

* * *

In Minneapolis, Dr. Rice was brought before the hospital superintendent on charges of using vulgarity to a Nurse Nicholas.

"Did you shout obscenities at this woman?" asked the superintendent. "Explain yourself."

"Well," said Rice, "this morning when my alarm rang, I got up to turn it off, tripped over the wire, broke the lamp and bruised my knee. As I was shaving the doorbell rang and I cut myself. The young fellow at the door was selling magazine subscriptions, and I had to buy three of them before I could get rid of him. By this time my coffee was cold and the toast was burnt. As I got into my car, I slipped on the ice and tore my pants. The car wouldn't start so I had to wait 40 minutes for road service. As I was pulling into the hospital parking lot, a taxi backed into my car and caused $800 worth of damage. I finally got to the fourth floor when Miss Nicholas came up to me and said, 'Doctor, I just received a shipment of thermometers, what should I do with them?' "

* * *

After purchasing a tie in a men's shop Doctor Greene took out his checkbook to write a check for it. He reached into his vest pocket and instead of a pen he pulled out a thermometer. He said, "I wonder what asshole has my pen?"

* * *

Amanda: Do I have Asian flu?
Doctor: No, you have Egyptian flu.
Amanda: What's that?
Doctor: You're going to become a mummy.

"Your boss is crazy, I can't find any lead!"

At 4:00 A.M. a doctor who practiced acupuncture was awakened by the telephone.

"Doctor," said the caller, "I can't sleep!"

"All right," said the yawning M.D., "take two needles and call me in the morning!"

* * *

A surgeon not famed for precision
Decided on self-circumcision
　　One slip of the knife
　　"Oh dear!" cried his wife,
"Our love life will need some revision!"

* * *

Sawyer sat in the doctor's office. "I have a friend who's got a venereal disease, and he wants to know if it's difficult to cure."

"It can be done," said the medic.

"Eh, my friend would like to know if it's very expensive."

"The fee can be suited to the client's ability to pay. It only takes a few months, and no one else will know."

"One other thing," said Sawyer, "my friend would like to know if the treatment hurts."

"I don't know," said the doctor. "Take out your friend's penis and let's see."

Dr. Kinney completed his examination of the teenage girl and took her mother aside. "I'm afraid," he said, "that your daughter has syphilis."

"Oh, my!" exclaimed the embarrassed woman. "Tell me, could she possibly have caught it in a public lavatory?"

"It's possible," replied the M.D., "but it would certainly have been uncomfortable."

* * *

Sowby and Pennock, two young G.P.'s, were discussing their patients.

"I've got a new one," said Sowby. "She's 22, has a body that won't quit. Boobs out to here and an ass just made for two hands."

"What's her problem?" asked Pennock.

"Every time she sneezes she has this wild urge to get laid."

"What are you giving her for it?"

"Black pepper."

* * *

Baldwin, a rich old man, consulted with a doctor. "I've been married three times and never had any children. I'm seeing a gorgeous young chickie who's 23 and anxious to be my bride. Here's what I want to know: If I marry her, do you think I'd be able to have an heir?"

"I'm sorry," said the doctor, "you may be heir-minded, but you're not heir-conditioned!"

* * *

The town busybody stopped Dr. Kendrick and wanted to know about Mrs. Callahan's new baby.

"The child was born without a penis," he said.

"Oh!" gasped the woman.

"But," added the doctor, "she'll have a damn nice place to put one in 20 years."

* * *

Lana, a really attractive Broadway show dancer, threw her knee completely out of joint. She went to a chiropractor. The doctor examined her and then quipped, "What's a joint like this doing in a pretty girl like you?"

* * *

Dr. Skinner was telling another doctor about his latest operation: "I grafted two beautiful boobs on a sailor's back."

"Was it a success?" asked the other surgeon.

"You kiddin'? I did it on a percentage basis. If his ass holds out, we'll both be millionaires."

Barry Heller, the handsome Harbor General Internist, gets guffaws telling this whopper:

Old Doc Williams had been serving his rural community in South Carolina for over 40 years. Now Farmer Reed's wife was due to give birth, and the country doctor was right there to help.

He and Reed were in the bedroom. "Hold the lantern up so I can see what I'm doing," said Williams.

Out came a baby.

Then another.

After the third baby the doctor said, "Better put out that lantern. I think that's what's attracting them."

Dr. Bradley's son was just graduated from Johns Hopkins Medical School, and he took him along on his daily rounds so that the young man could learn more about diagnosis. In one of the sickrooms they visited, the father advised the patient, "You're smoking too much, Mr. Forbes. You'll have to stop."

"You're right, Doc," he admitted. "I'll give it up."

When the two physicians left the house, the son said, "How'd you diagnose that so quickly?"

"Observation. I saw cigar bands on the floor and ashes in the wastepaper basket. Now, on the next case, you take over."

At the house the son looked the woman over, then advised, "Mrs. Grant you'll save yourself a lot of problems if you stop drinking milk."

"You're right, Doctor," she nodded.

When the pair stepped out onto the street, the father said, "That was excellent, son, how did you reach that diagnosis?"

"From under the bed I saw the milkman's feet sticking out!"

* * *

Dr. Perlman was examining a patient when his nurse rushed into the room. "Excuse me, Doctor," she said, "but that man you just gave a clean bill of health to walked out of the office and dropped dead. What should I do?"

"Turn him around so he looks like he was walking in," replied the M.D.

* * *

Marianne, a newlywed, complained of her husband's terrific snoring. Her physician advised, "When he falls asleep, pull his legs apart."

To her surprise, it worked. On her next visit she begged the M.D. to explain. "When you pulled his legs apart," said the doctor, "his testicles dropped down over his ass and cut off the draft."

* * *

"Doctor," said the pretty model, "I have this compulsion to go to bed with every man I meet. Is there a name for whatever it is I've got?"

"Yes, there is," replied the medical man as he picked her up and carried her over to the couch. "It's called good news!"

* * *

The mother complained to Dr. Randall that her son Ezra was continually masturbating.

"Why do you do it?" asked the physician.

"I'm bored," said the youngster. "I got nothin' to do. I hate TV and I hate sports, so I jerk off!"

Randall sent Ezra to the waiting room so he could discuss the situation with his mother. Fifteen minutes later, they went into the waiting room and found the place strewn with candy wrappers.

"What have you been doing?" asked the doctor.

"Eatin' these candies," replied Ezra.

"What?" said the doctor. "I had a five pound box of candy there. Did you eat the entire box?"

"Sure. I was bored," said the boy. "I had nothin' to do."

"You meathead!" shouted the doctor. "Why didn't you go home and masturbate!"

* * *

ALLERGY SPECIALIST—*A doctor who treats you for one wheezin' or another.*

ANALYST—*A shrink trying to find out whether an infant has more fun in infancy than an adult in adultery.*

ARTIFICIAL INSEMINATION—*Copulation without representation; inoculate conception.*

BISEXUAL—*A man who likes girls as well as the next fellow.*

CHIROPODIST—*Makes money hand over foot; a guy who foots the bill.*

COLD—*It's like a committee meeting—sometimes the eyes have it, and sometimes the nose.*

CONSULTATION—*A medical term meaning share the wealth.*

DENTIST—*A man who lives from hand to mouth.*

DIAGNOSIS—*A preface to an autopsy.*

DRUGGIST—*A man in a white coat who stands behind a soda fountain and sells ballpoint pens.*

DOCTOR—*A person who acts like a humanitarian and charges like a TV repairman.*

DOCTOR'S WIFE—*The only one who knows when the doctor is in at night.*

DYSPEPSIA—*Remorse of a guilty stomach.*

ENEMA—*A goose with a gush.*

GYNECOLOGIST—*A private's investigator; a spreader of old wives' tails; a doctor who, when he dates a girl, people never have to wonder what he sees in her.*

HALITOSIS—*A breath that takes yours away.*

HEMATOLOGIST—*The opposite of a urologist, he's a doctor who pricks your finger.*

HOSPITALS—*Places where people who are run down wind up; where men keep asking their nurses for dates and the nurses keep giving them prunes.*

HOSPITAL ROOM—*A place where friends of the patient go to talk to other friends of the patient.*

HYMEN—*A greeting to male companions.*

HYPOCHONDRIAC—*One who can't leave being well alone; one who won't even talk on the phone to anybody who has a cold.*

ILLEGIBLE—*Doctor's prescription.*

MALE MENOPAUSE—*Change of wife*

MANIC DEPRESSIVE—*A person whose philosophy is: easy glum, easy glow.*

MEDICINE CHEST—*Drugstore without sandwiches.*

NEURASTHENIC—*A person who is always on pins and needles.*

NYMPHOMANIA—*Aye trouble; one disease where the patient enjoys being bedridden.*

OBSTETRICIAN—*One who takes out for money what another man has put in for fun.*

OSTEOPATH—*One who works his fingers to the bone.*

ORGASM—*The grand finale.*

ORGASMIC IMPOTENCE—*When the spurt is unwilling and the flesh is weak.*

PANSY PROCTOLOGIST—*A doctor who can pack your hemorrhoids with both his hands on your shoulders.*

PANSY PSYCHIATRIST—*He goes around shrinking heads—sometimes three or four in one night.*

PENICILLIN—*What you give the man who has everything.*

187

PROCTOLOGIST—*A super duper pooper snooper.*

PROCTOSCOPE—*A long thing you look through with an asshole at each end.*

PSYCHIATRIST—*A trauma critic.*

PSYCHOANALYST—*One who stops you from worrying about your problem and starts you worrying about your bill; a person who reads between the lines even when there is nothing there; someone who can take any simple problem and explain it in language nobody can understand.*

PSYCHOLOGIST—*A man who watches everybody else when a pretty girl enters the room.*

RHEUMATISM—*Nature's first weather bureau.*

SEX DRIVE—*Trying to find a motel that has a vacancy.*

SODOMY—*Rump hump.*

SOUTHERN PSYCHIATRIST—*One who prefers Freud chicken.*

SPECIALIST—*A doctor whose patients are expected to confine their ailments to office hours; a doctor with a smaller practice but a bigger yacht.*

SPECIMEN—*An Italian astronaut.*

VIRGIN—*A girl who hasn't met her maker.*

* * *

ABOUT THE AUTHOR

This is the 22nd humor collection produced by comedian Larry Wilde. His *Official* joke books with sales over 5,000,000 represent the largest selling humor series in publishing annals.

Mr. Wilde has also authored two books considered to be the definitive works on comedic technique: THE GREAT COMEDIANS and HOW THE GREAT COMEDY WRITERS CREATE LAUGHTER.

Born in Jersey City, New Jersey, Larry Wilde spent two years in the U.S. Marine Corps and graduated from the University of Miami, Florida. He worked his way through school, appearing at Miami Beach hotels and clubs.

Mr. Wilde has entertained in the country's finest night spots and on television in sitcoms and commercials. Recognized as America's foremost humor authority, he is also in great demand on the lecture circuit.

Larry is married to the former Maryruth Poulos, a Wyoming music major who has just completed her first book: THE BEST OF ETHNIC HOME COOKING (*J.P. Tarcher*).

The couple reside in Los Angeles.

BOOKS BY LARRY WILDE

More THE OFFICIAL SEX MANIACS JOKE BOOK
THE *Last* OFFICIAL JEWISH JOKE BOOK
also

THE OFFICIAL BEDROOM/BATHROOM
  JOKE BOOK
More THE OFFICIAL DEMOCRAT/REPUBLICAN
  JOKE BOOK
More THE OFFICIAL SMART KIDS/DUMB
  PARENTS JOKE BOOK
THE OFFICIAL BOOK OF SICK JOKES
More THE OFFICIAL JEWISH/IRISH JOKE BOOK
THE *Last* OFFICIAL ITALIAN JOKE BOOK
THE OFFICIAL CAT LOVERS/DOG LOVERS
  JOKE BOOK
THE OFFICIAL DIRTY JOKE BOOK
THE *Last* OFFICIAL POLISH JOKE BOOK
THE OFFICIAL GOLFERS JOKE BOOK
THE OFFICIAL SMART KIDS/DUMB PARENTS
  JOKE BOOK
THE OFFICIAL RELIGIOUS/*Not So* RELIGIOUS
  JOKE BOOK
THE OFFICIAL DEMOCRAT/REPUBLICAN
  JOKE BOOK
More THE OFFICIAL POLISH/ITALIAN
  JOKE BOOK
THE OFFICIAL BLACK FOLKS/WHITE FOLKS
  JOKE BOOK
THE OFFICIAL VIRGINS/SEX MANIACS
  JOKE BOOK
THE OFFICIAL JEWISH/IRISH JOKE BOOK
THE OFFICIAL POLISH/ITALIAN JOKE BOOK

and

THE COMPLETE BOOK OF ETHNIC HUMOR
  (Corwin)
HOW THE GREAT COMEDY WRITERS CREATE
LAUGHTER (Nelson-Hall)
THE GREAT COMEDIANS (Citadel Press)

DOONESBURY

G. B. Trudeau's comics are the nation's most popular and beloved cartoons. Doonesbury is the first comic strip to win the Pulitzer Prize. Now you can enjoy these mirthful, biting chronicles of our times featuring the relentless Doonesbury crowd.

THE LATEST BOOKS IN THE BANTAM BESTSELLING TRADITION

☐	14512	**NO LOVE LOST** Helen van Slyke	$3.75
☐	01328	**TIDES OF LOVE** Patricia Matthews (Large Format)	$5.95
☐	13545	**SOPHIE'S CHOICE** William Styron	$3.50
☐	14200	**PRINCESS DAISY** Judith Krantz	$3.95
☐	20025	**THE FAR PAVILIONS** M. M. Kaye	$4.50
☐	14068	**THE CANADIANS: BLACK ROBE** Robert E. Wall	$2.95
☐	13752	**SHADOW OF THE MOON** M. M. Kaye	$3.95
☐	14249	**CHILDREN OF THE LION** Peter Danielson	$2.95
☐	13980	**TEXAS!** Dana Fuller Ross	$2.75
☐	14968	**THE RENEGADE** Donald Clayton Porter	$2.95
☐	20087	**THE HAWK AND THE DOVE** Leigh Franklin James	$2.95
☐	13641	**PORTRAITS** Cynthia Freeman	$3.50
☐	20670	**FAIRYTALES** Cynthia Freeman	$3.50
☐	14439	**THE EWINGS OF DALLAS** Burt Hirschfeld	$2.75
☐	13992	**CHANTAL** Claire Lorrimer	$2.95

Buy them at your local bookstore or use this handy coupon:

Bantam Books, Inc., Dept. FBS, 414 East Golf Road, Des Plaines, Ill. 60016

Please send me the books I have checked below. I am enclosing $_____ (please add $1.00 to cover postage and handling). Send check or money order —no cash or C.O.D.'s please.

Mr/Mrs/Miss_____

Address_____

City_____ State/Zip_____

FBS—7/81

Please allow four to six weeks for delivery. This offer expires 1/82.

Bantam Book Catalog

Here's your up-to-the-minute listing of over 1,400 titles by your favorite authors.

This illustrated, large format catalog gives a description of each title. For your convenience, it is divided into categories in fiction and non-fiction—gothics, science fiction, westerns, mysteries, cookbooks, mysticism and occult, biographies, history, family living, health, psychology, art.

So don't delay—take advantage of this special opportunity to increase your reading pleasure.

Just send us your name and address and 50¢ (to help defray postage and handling costs).